Berlitz®

Italia

phrase book & dictionary

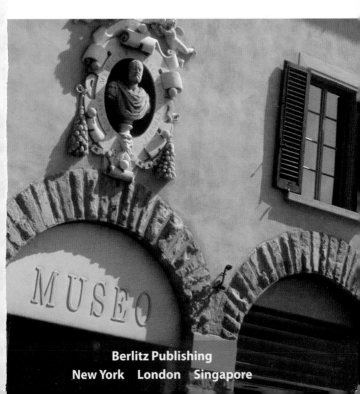

MUSEO

Berlitz Publishing
New York   London   Singapore

Contacting the Editors

Every effort has been made to provide accurate information in this publication, but changes are inevitable. The publisher cannot be responsible for any resulting loss, inconvenience or injury. We would appreciate it if readers would call our attention to any errors or outdated information. We also welcome your suggestions; if you come across a relevant expression not in our phrase book, please contact us at: **comments@berlitzpublishing.com**

All Rights Reserved
© 2007 APA Publications (UK) Ltd.
Berlitz Trademark Reg. U.S. Patent Office and other countries. Marca Registrada. Used under license from Berlitz Investment Corporation.

Eleventh Printing: March 2012
Printed in China

Publishing Director: Mina Patria
Commissioning Editor: Kate Drynan
Editorial Assistant: Sophie Cooper
Translation: updated by Wordbank
Cover Design: Beverley Speight
Interior Design: Beverley Speight
Production Manager: Raj Trivedi
Picture Researcher: Lucy Johnston
Cover Photo: All photos Britta Jaschinski/APA except 'currency' photo Lucy Johnston/APA.

Interior Photos: All photography Britta Jaschinski/APA except Kevin Cummins/APA 38; iStockphoto 131, 134, 138, 148, 149, 152; Lucy Johnston/APA 16, 174; Susan Smart/APA 107, 110, 126, 140, 144.

Contents

Food & Drink

People

Leisure Time

Special Requirements

In an Emergency

Dictionary

Pronunciation

This section is designed to make you familiar with the sounds of Italian using our simplified phonetic transcription. You'll find the pronunciation of the Italian letters and sounds explained below, together with their 'imitated' equivalents. This system is used throughout the phrase book; simply read the pronunciation as if it were English, noting any special rules below.

Stress has been indicated in the phonetic pronunciations by underlining. These letters should be pronounced with more emphasis. Generally, the vowel of the next to last syllable is stressed. When a final vowel is stressed, it has an accent.

Consonants

Letter(s)	Approximate Pronunciation	Symbol	Example	Pronunciation
c	1. before e and i, ch as in chip	ch	**cerco**	_chehr_•koh
	2. elsewhere, c as in cat	k	**conto**	_kohn_•toh
ch	c as in cat	k	**che**	keh
g	1. before e and i, like j in jet	j	**valigia**	vah•_lee_•jyah
	2. elsewhere, g as in go	g	**grande**	_grahn_•deh
gg	pronounced more intensely	dj	**viaggio**	_vyah_•djoh
gh	g as in go	gh	**ghiaccio**	_ghyah_•chyoh
gli	lli as in million	lly	**bagaglio**	bah•_gah_•llyoh
gn	like the first n in onion	ny	**bagno**	_bah_•nyoh
h	always silent		**ha**	ah

Letter(s)	Approximate Pronunciation	Symbol	Example	Pronunciation
r	rolled in the back of the mouth	r	**Roma**	_roh·mah_
s	1. generally s as in sit	s	**salsa**	_sahl·sah_
	2. sometimes z as in zoo	z	**casa**	_kah·zah_
sc	1. before e and i, sh as in shut	sh	**uscita**	_oo·shee·tah_
	2. elsewhere, sk as in skin	sk	**scarpa**	_skahr·pah_
z/zz	1. generally ts as in hits	ts	**grazie**	_grah·tsyeh_
	2. sometimes a little softer, like dz	dz	**zero**	_dzeh·roh_

The letters b, d, f, k, l, m, n, p, q, t and v are pronounced as in English. The letters j, k, w, x and y are not true members of the Italian alphabet and appear only in foreign words or names.

Vowels

Letter	Approximate Pronunciation	Symbol	Example	Pronunciation
a	short, as in father	ah	**gatto**	_gaht·toh_
e	1. like e as in get	eh	**destra**	_deh·strah_
	2. before a single consonant, sometimes like e in they	ay	**sete**	_say·teh_

Letter	Approximate Pronunciation	Symbol	Example	Pronunciation
i	ee as in meet	**ee**	**vini**	_vee•nee_
o	o as in so	**oh**	**sole**	_soh•leh_
u	oo as in boot	**oo**	**fumo**	_foo•moh_

Vowel Combinations

Letter	Symbol	Example	Pronunciation
ae	**ah•eh**	**paese**	_pah•eh•zeh_
ao	**ah•oh**	**Paolo**	_pah•oh•loh_
au	**ow**	**auto**	_ow•toh_
eo	**eh•oh**	**museo**	_moo•zeh•oh_
eu	**eh•oo**	**euro**	_eh•oo•roh_
ei	**ay**	**lei**	_lay_
ia	**yah**	**piazza**	_pyah•tsah_
ie	**yeh**	**piede**	_pyeh•deh_
io	**yoh**	**piove**	_pyoh•veh_
iu	**yoo**	**più**	_pyoo_
ua	**wah**	**quale**	_kwah•leh_
ue	**weh**	**questo**	_kweh•stoh_
ui	**wee**	**qui**	_kwee_
uo	**woh**	**può**	_pwoh_

There are approximately 60 million Italian speakers. Many different dialects add variety and color to the country's linguistic landscape. In addition, Italian is spoken in the southern area of Switzerland.

How to use this Book

> Sometimes you see two alternatives separated by a slash. Choose the one that's right for your situation.

ESSENTIAL

I'm on vacation [holiday]/business.

Sono in vacanza/viaggio d'affari.
soh•noh een vah•kahn•tsah/vyah•djoh dahf•fah•ree

I'm going to...

Vado a ... *vah•doh ah ...*

I'm staying at the...Hotel.

Sono all'hotel ... *soh•noh ahl•loh•tehl ...*

> Words you may see are shown in YOU MAY SEE boxes.

YOU MAY SEE...

DOGANA	customs
MERCE DUTY-FREE	duty-free goods
MERCE DA DICHIARARE	goods to declare

> Any of the words or phrases listed can be plugged into the sentence below.

Tickets

When's the...to Milan?

A che ora è il/l'...per Milano? *ah keh oh•rah eh eel/l...pehr mee•lah•noh*

(first) bus

(primo) autobus *(pree•moh) ow•toh•boos*

(next) flight

(prossimo) volo *(prohs•see•moh) voh•loh*

(last) train

(ultimo) treno *(ool•tee•moh) treh•noh*

Italian phrases appear in purple.

Read the simplified pronunciation as if it were English. For more on pronunciation, see page 7.

Personal

Who are you with?   **Con chi è?** *kohn kee ee*.
I'm here alone.   **Sono da solo** *m* **/sola** *f*.
soh•noh dah soh•loh /soh•lah

When's your   **Quando è il suo compleanno?**
birthday?   *kwahn•doh eh eel soo•oh kohm•pleh•ahn•noh*

For Grammar, see page 162.

Related phrases can be found by going to the page number indicated.

When different gender forms apply, the masculine form is followed by *m*; feminine by *f*

A handshake is a common gesture among strangers or in formal settings. Traditionally, it is expected that a woman be the first to offer her hand. A kiss on both cheeks is used among friends and relatives. A nod and a smile suffice when greeting members of a group of people.

Information boxes contain relevant country, culture and language tips.

Expressions you may hear are shown in You May Hear boxes.

YOU MAY HEAR...

Parlo poco inglese. *pahr•loh poh•koh een•gleh•zeh*   I only speak a little English.
Non parlo inglese. *nohn pahr•loh een•gleh•zeh*   I don't speak English.

Color-coded side bars identify each section of the book.

Survival

Arrival & Departure

ESSENTIAL

I'm on vacation [holiday]/business. **Sono in vacanza/viaggio d'affari.** _soh•noh een vah•kahn•tsah/vyah•djoh dahf•fah•ree_

I'm going to... **Vado a...** _vah•doh ah..._

I'm staying at the...Hotel. **Sono all'hotel...** _soh•noh ahl•loh•tehl..._

YOU MAY HEAR...

Il passaporto, per favore. _eel pahs•sah•pohr•toh pehr fah•voh•reh_ — Your passport, please.

Motivo della visita? _moh•tee•voh dehl•lah vee•zee•tah_ — What's the purpose of your visit?

Dove alloggia? _doh•veh ahl•loh•djah_ — Where are you staying?

Quanto tempo si ferma? _kwahn•toh tehm•poh see fehr•mah_ — How long are you staying?

Chi viaggia con Lei? _kee vyah•djah kohn lay_ — Who are you traveling with?

Per favore is the standard Italian translation for 'please.'
Prego is the standard Italian translation for 'you are welcome,' but it's also used for 'please,' in the sense of 'if you please,' in certain informal situations.

Border Control

I'm just passing through.	**Sono solo di passaggio.** _soh·noh soh·loh dee pahs·sah·djoh_
I'd like to declare…	**Vorrei dichiarare…** _vohr·ray dee·kyah·rah·reh_…
I have nothing to declare.	**Non ho nulla da dichiarare.** _nohn oh nool·lah dah dee·kyah·rah·reh_

YOU MAY HEAR…

Ha qualcosa da dichiarare?
ah kwahl·koh·zah dah dee·kyah·rah·reh

Anything to declare?

Deve pagare la tassa su questo. _deh·veh pah·gah·reh lah tahs·sah soo kweh·stoh_

You must pay duty on this.

Apra questa borsa. _ah·prah kweh·stah bohr·sah_

Open this bag.

YOU MAY SEE…

DOGANA	customs
MERCE DUTY-FREE	duty-free goods
MERCE DA DICHIARARE	goods to declare
NULLA DA DICHIARARE	nothing to declare
CONTROLLO PASSAPORTI	passport control
POLIZIA	police

Money

ESSENTIAL

Where's…?	**Dov'è…?** doh•_veh_…
the ATM	**il bancomat** eel _bahn_•koh•maht
the bank	**la banca** lah _bahn_•kah
the currency exchange office	**l'ufficio di cambio** loof•_fee_•chyoh dee _kahm_•byoh
When does the bank open/close?	**A che ora apre/chiude la banca?** ah keh _oh_•rah _ah_•preh/_kyoo_•deh lah _bahn_•kah
I'd like to change dollars/pounds into euros.	**Vorrei cambiare dei dollari/delle sterline in euro.** vohr•_ray_ kahm•_byah_•reh day _dohl_•lah•ree/_dehl_•leh stehr•_lee_•neh een _eh_•oo•roh
I'd like to cash traveler's checks [cheques].	**Vorrei riscuotere dei travellers cheques.** vohr•_ray_ ree•skwoh•_teh_•reh day _trah_•vehl•lehrs chehks

At the Bank

I'd like to change money.	**Vorrei cambiare del denaro.** *vohr·ray kahm·byah·reh dehl deh·nah·roh*
How much is the fee?	**Quant'è la commissione?** *kwahn·teh lah kohm·mees·syoh·neh*
I lost my traveler's checks [cheques]/ credit card.	**Ho perso i miei travellers cheques/ la mia carta di credito.** *oh pehr·soh ee mee·ay trah·vehl·lehrs chehks/lah mee·ah kahr·tah dee kreh·dee·toh*
My card was stolen/doesn't work.	**La mia carta di credito è stata rubata/non funziona.** *lah mee·ah kahr·tah dee kreh·dee·toh eh stah·tah roo·bah·tah/nohn foon·tsyoh·nah*

YOU MAY SEE…

Italian currency is the **euro €**, divided into 100 **centesimi**.
Coins: 1, 2, 5, 10, 20, 50 **cent**.; €1, 2
Notes: €5, 10, 20, 50, 100, 200, 500

YOU MAY SEE…

INSERIRE LA CARTA	insert card here
ANNULLA	cancel
CANCELLA	clear
CONFERMA	enter
CODICE SEGRETO	PIN
PRELIEVO	withdrawal
DEPOSITO	deposit
DA CONTO CORRENTE	from checking [current] account
DA CONTO DI RISPARMIO	from savings account
RICEVUTA	receipt

Cash can be obtained from ATMs with Visa™, Eurocard™, American Express® and many other international cards. Instructions are usually available in English. You can change money at travel agencies and hotels, but the rate will not be as good as at a bank or currency exchange office. Remember to bring your passport when you want to change money.

Getting Around

ESSENTIAL

How do I get to town?	**Come si arriva in città?** _koh·meh see ahr·ree·vah een cheet·tah_
Where's...?	**Dov'è...?** _doh·veh..._
the airport	**l'aeroporto** _lah·eh·roh·pohr·toh_
the train [railway] station	**la stazione ferroviaria** _lah stah·tsyoh·neh fehr·roh·vyah·ryah_
the bus station	**la stazione degli autobus** _lah stah·tsyoh·neh deh·llyee ow·toh·boos_
the metro [underground] station	**la stazione della metropolitana** _lah stah·tsyoh·neh dehl·lah meh·troh·poh·lee·tah·nah_
How far is it?	**Quanto dista?** _kwahn·toh dees·tah_
Where do I buy a ticket?	**Dove si comprano i biglietti?** _doh·veh see kohm·prah·noh ee bee·llyeht·tee_
A one-way/ return-trip ticket to...	**Un biglietto di andata/di andata e ritorno per...** _oon bee·llyeht·toh dee ahn·dah·tah/ dee ahn·dah·tah eh ree·tohr·noh pehr..._
How much?	**Quant'è?** _kwahn·teh_
Is there a discount?	**C'è uno sconto?** _cheh oon·oh skohn·toh_
Which...?	**Quale...?** _kwah·leh..._
gate	**uscita** _oo·shee·tah_
line	**linea** _lee·neh·ah_
platform	**binario** _bee·nah·ryoh_
Where can I get a taxi?	**Dove posso trovare un taxi?** _doh·veh pohs·soh troh·vah·reh oon tah·ksee_

Take me to this address.	**Mi porti a questo indirizzo.** *mee pohr·tee ah kweh·stoh een·dee·ree·tsoh*
Where's the car rental [hire]?	**Dov'è un autonoleggio?** *doh·veh oon ow·toh·noh·leh·djoh*
Can I have a map?	**Può darmi una cartina?** *pwoh dahr·mee oo·nah kahr·tee·nah*

Tickets

When's the...to Milan?	**A che ora è il/l'...per Milano?** *ah keh oh·rah eh eel/l...pehr mee·lah·noh*
(first) bus	**(primo) autobus** *(pree·moh) ow·toh·boos*
(next) flight	**(prossimo) volo** *(prohs·see·moh) voh·loh*
(last) train	**(ultimo) treno** *(ool·tee·moh) treh·noh*
Where do I buy a ticket?	**Dove si comprano i biglietti?** *doh·veh see kohm·prah·noh ee bee·llyeht·tee*
One/Two ticket(s), please.	**Un biglietto/Due biglietti, per favore.** *oon bee·llyeht·toh/doo·eh bee·llyeht·tee pehr fah·voh·reh*
For today/tomorrow.	**Per oggi/domani.** *pehr oh·djee/doh·mah·nee*
A...ticket.	**Un biglietto...** *oon bee·llyeht·toh...*
one-way	**di andata** *dee ahn·dah·tah*
return-trip	**di andata e ritorno** *dee ahn·dah·tah eh ree·tohr·noh*
first class	**di prima classe** *dee pree·mah klahs·seh*
business class	**Biglietti di business class** *bee·llyeht·tee dee beez·nehs klahs*
second class	**di seconda classe** *dee seh·kohn·dah klahs·seh*
economy class	**di classe economica** *dee klahs·seh eh·koh·noh·mee·kah*
How much?	**Quant'è?** *kwahn·teh*

per l'anzione

Is there a...	**C'è un biglietto ridotto per...?** *cheh oon*
discount?	*bee·llyeht·toh ree·doht·toh pehr...*
child	**bambini** *bahm·bee·nee*
student	**studenti** *stoo·dehn·tee*
senior citizen	**anziani** *ahn·tsyah·nee*
tourist	**turisti** *too·ree·stee*

The express/local
bus/train, please.
L'autobus/Il treno espresso/locale, per favore.
*low·toh·boos/eel treh·noh eh·sprehs·soh/
loh·kah·leh pehr fah·voh·reh*

I have an e-ticket.
Ho un biglietto elettronico. *oh oon bee·llyeht·toh
eh·leht·troh·nee·koh*

Can I buy a ticket
on the bus/train?
**Posso comprare il biglietto sull'autobus/
sul treno?** *pohs·soh kohm·prah·reh eel bee·llyeht·toh
sool·low·toh·boos/sool treh·noh*

Do I have to stamp
the ticket before
boarding?
**Devo obliterare/timbrare il biglietto prima
di salire a bordo?** *deh·voh
oh·blee·teh·rah·reh/teem·brah·reh eel bee·llyeht·toh
pree·mah dee sah·lee·reh ah bohr·doh?*

How long is this
ticket valid?
Per quanto tempo è valido questo biglietto?
*pehr kwahn·toh tehm·poh eh vah·lee·doh kweh·stoh
bee·llyeht·toh*

Can I return on the
same ticket?
**Posso fare il viaggio di ritorno con lo stesso
biglietto?** *pohs·soh fah·reh eel vyah·djoh dee
ree·tohr·noh kohn loh stehs·soh bee·llyeht·toh*

I'd like to...my
reservation.
Vorrei...la prenotazione. *vohr·ray...lah
preh·noh·tah·tsyoh·neh*

cancel	**annullare** *ahn·nool·lah·reh*
change	**cambiare** *kahm·byah·reh*
confirm	**confermare** *kohn·fehr·mah·reh*

For Days, see page 169.
For Time, see page 169.

Plane

Airport Transfer

How much is a taxi to the airport?	**Quant'è la tariffa del taxi fino all'aeroporto?** *kwahn·teh lah tah·reef·fah dehl tah·ksee fee·noh ahl·lah·eh·roh·pohr·toh*
To...Airport, please.	**All'aeroporto di..., per favore.** *ahl·lah·eh·roh·pohr·toh dee... pehr fah·voh·reh*
My airline is...	**Parto con la/l'...** *pahr·toh kohn lah/l...*
My flight leaves at...	**Il volo è alle...** *eel voh·loh eh ahl·leh...*
I'm in a rush.	**Ho fretta.** *oh freht·tah*
Can you take an alternate route?	**Può prendere un'altra strada?** *pwoh prehn·deh·reh oo·nahl·trah strah·dah*
Can you drive faster/slower?	**Può andare più velocemente/lentamente?** *pwoh ahn·dah·reh pyoo veh·loh·cheh·mehn·teh/ lehn·tah·mehn·teh*

YOU MAY HEAR...

Con che compagnia aerea viaggia? *kohn keh kohm·pah·nee·ah ah·eh·reh·ah vyah·djah*	What airline are you flying?
Nazionale o internazionale? *nah·tsyoh·nah·leh oh een·tehr·nah·tsyoh·nah·leh*	Domestic or international?
Quale terminal? *kwah·leh tehr·mee·nahl*	What terminal?

Checking In

Where's check-in?	**Dov'è il check-in?** *doh·veh eel chehk·een*
My name is...	**Mi chiamo...** *mee kyah·moh...*
I'm going to...	**Vado a...** *vah·doh ah...*

YOU MAY SEE…

ARRIVI	arrivals
PARTENZE	departures
RITIRO BAGAGLI	baggage claim
SICUREZZA	security
VOLI NAZIONALI	domestic flights
VOLI INTERNAZIONALI	international flights
CHECK-IN	check-in
CHECK-IN CON BIGLIETTO ELETTRONICO	e-ticket check-in
USCITA	exit

I have…	**Ho** *oh*
one suitcase	**una valigia** *oo·nah vah·lee·jyah*
two suitcases	**due valigie** *doo·eh vah·lee·jyeh*
one piece of hand luggage	**un bagaglio a mano** *oon bah·gah·llyoh ah mah·noh*
How much luggage is allowed?	**Quanti bagagli si possono portare?** *kwahn·tee bah·<u>gah</u>·llyee see pohs·soh·noh pohr·<u>tah</u>·reh*
Is that pounds or kilos?	**È in libbre o in chili?** *eh een leeb·breh oh een kee·lee*
Which terminal/gate?	**Quale terminal/uscita?** *<u>kwah</u>·leh tehr·mee·<u>nahl</u>/oo·<u>shee</u>·tah*
I'd like a window/an aisle seat.	**Vorrei un posto vicino al finestrino/al corridoio.** *vohr·<u>ray</u> oon <u>poh</u>·stoh vee·<u>chee</u>·noh ahl fee·neh·<u>stree</u>·noh/ahl kohr·ree·<u>doh</u>·yoh*
When do we leave/arrive?	**Quando partiamo/arriviamo?** *<u>kwahn</u>·doh pahr·<u>tyah</u>·moh/ahr·ree·<u>vyah</u>·moh*
Is the flight delayed?	**Il volo è in ritardo?** *eel <u>voh</u>·loh eh een ree·<u>tahr</u>·doh*
How late?	**Di quanto è in ritardo?** *dee <u>kwahn</u>·toh eh een ree·<u>tahr</u>·doh*

Luggage

Where is/Where are...?	**Dov'è/Dove sono...?** *doh·veh/doh·veh soh·noh...*	
the luggage carts [trolleys]	**i carrelli per i bagagli** *ee kahr·rehl·lee pehr ee bah·gah·llyee*	
the luggage lockers	**il deposito bagagli** *eel deh·poh·see·toh bah·gah·llyee*	

YOU MAY HEAR...

Il prossimo! *eel prohs·see·moh*
Next!

Il suo passaporto/biglietto, per favore.
eel soo·oh pahs·sah·pohr·toh/bee·llyeht·toh pehr fah·voh·reh
Your passport/ticket, please.

Quanti bagagli consegna? *kwahn·tee bah·gah·llyee kohn·seh·nyah*
How many bags are you checking?

Ha il bagaglio in eccesso. *ah eel bah·gah·llyoh een eh·chehs·soh*
You have excess luggage.

È troppo grande per portarlo a mano.
eh trohp·poh grahn·deh pehr pohr·tahr·loh ah mah·noh
That's too large for a carry-on [piece of hand luggage].

Ha fatto Lei le valigie? *ah faht·toh lay leh vah·lee·jyeh*
Did you pack these bags yourself?

Qualcuno le ha dato qualcosa da portare?
kwahl·koo·noh leh ah dah·toh kwahl·koh·zah dah pohr·tah·reh
Did anyone give you anything to carry?

Vuoti le tasche. *vwoh·tee leh tahs·keh*
Empty your pockets.

Tolga le scarpe. *tohl·gah leh skahr·peh*
Take off your shoes.

Imbarco immediato... *eem·bahr·koh eem·meh·dyah·toh...*
Now boarding...

the baggage claim	**il ritiro bagagli** *eel ree·tee·roh bah·gah·llyee*
My luggage has been lost/stolen.	**Mi hanno perso/rubato i bagagli.** *mee ahn·noh pehr·soh/roo·bah·toh ee bah·gah·llyee*
My suitcase has been damaged.	**La mia valigia è danneggiata.** *lah mee·ah vah·lee·jyah eh dahn·neh·djah·tah*

Finding your Way

Where is/Where are…?	**Dov'è/Dove sono…?** *doh·veh/doh·veh soh·noh…*
the currency exchange	**il cambio valuta** *eel kahm·byoh vah·loo·tah*
the car rental [hire]	**l'autonoleggio** *l·ow·toh·noh·leh·djoh*
the exit	**l'uscita** *loo·shee·tah*
the taxis	**i taxi** *ee tah·ksee*
Is there… into town?	**C'è…per andare in città?** *cheh…pehr ahn·dah·reh een cheet·tah*
a bus	**un autobus** *oon ow·toh·boos*
a train	**un treno** *oon treh·noh*
a subway [underground]	**una metropolitana** *oo·nah meh·troh·poh·lee·tah·nah*

For Asking Directions, see page 33.

Train

Where's the train [railway] station?	**Dov'è la stazione ferroviaria?** *doh·veh lah stah·tsyoh·neh fehr·roh·vyah·ryah*
How far is it?	**Quanto dista?** *kwahn·toh dees·tah*
Where is/ Where are…?	**Dov'è/Dove sono…?** *doh·veh/doh·veh soh·noh…*
the ticket office	**la biglietteria** *lah bee·llyeht·teh·ree·ah*
the information	**l'ufficio informazioni** *loof·fee·chyoh*

YOU MAY SEE...

BINARI	platforms
INFORMAZIONI	information
PRENOTAZIONI	reservations
SALA D'ATTESA	waiting room
ARRIVI	arrivals
PARTENZE	departures

desk	*een·fohr·mah·tsyoh·nee*
the luggage	**il deposito bagagli** *eel deh·poh·see·toh*
lockers	*bah·gah·llyee*
the platforms	**i binari** *ee bee·nah·ree*
Can I have a	**Mi può dare un orario?** *mee pwoh dah·reh* ✔
schedule [timetable]?	*oon oh·rah·ryoh*
How long is	**Quanto dura il viaggio?** *kwahn·toh doo·rah* ✔
the trip?	*eel vyah·djoh*
Do I have to	**Devo cambiare?** *deh·voh kahm·byah·reh* ✔
change trains?	

For Asking Directions, see page 33.

For Tickets, see page 19.

Rail travel is extremely popular and one of the best ways to see
Italy, especially with the faster—and more expensive—trains
that link major cities. **Eurostar** and **InterCity** are the fastest trains,
while **diretti**, **regionali** and **interregionali** are local trains—ideal
to reach smaller towns. Tickets must be stamped before travel in one of
the many machines on station concourses and platforms.

Italians use the 24-hour clock in schedules and other official documents and situations. In other words, the morning hours from 1:00 a.m. to 12:00 noon are the same as in English; after that, just add 12. So, 1:00 p.m. would be 13:00, 5:00 p.m. would be 17:00 and so on.

Departures

Which track [platform] to…?	**Da che binario parte il treno per…?** *dah keh bee-nah-ryoh pahr-teh eel treh-noh pehr…*
Is this the track [platform]/train to…?	**È il binario/treno per…?** *eh eel bee-nah-ryoh/ treh-noh pehr…*
Where is track [platform]…?	**Dov'è il binario…?** *doh-veh eel bee-nah-ryoh…*
Where do I change for…?	**Dove devo cambiare per…?** *doh-veh deh-voh kahm-byah-reh pehr…*

On Board

Can I sit here/open the window?	**Posso sedermi qui/aprire il finestrino?** *pohs-soh seh-dehr-mee kwee/ah-pree-reh eel fee-neh-stree-noh*
That's my seat.	**Questo posto è mio.** *kweh-stoh poh-stoh eh mee-oh*
Here's my reservation.	**Ecco la mia prenotazione** *ek-koh lah mee-ah preh-noh-tah-tsyoh-neh*

Bus

Where's the bus station?	**Dov'è la stazione degli autobus?** *doh-veh lah stah-tsyoh-neh deh-llyee ow-toh-boos*
How far is it?	**Quanto dista?** *kwahn-toh dees-tah*
How do I get to…?	**Come si arriva a…?** *koh-meh see ahr-ree-vah ah…*
Is this the bus to…?	**È l'autobus per…?** *eh low-toh-boos pehr…*
Can you tell me when to get off?	**Può dirmi quando scendere?** *pwoh deer-mee kwahn-doh shehn-deh-reh*

YOU MAY HEAR...

Biglietti, per favore. bee-_llyeht_-tee pehr
fah-_voh_-reh

Tickets, please.

Deve cambiare a Parma. _deh_-veh
kahm-_byah_-reh ah _pahr_-mah

You have to change
at Parma.

Prossima fermata: Pisa. _prohs_-see-mah
fehr-_mah_-tah _pee_-zah

Next stop, Pisa.

Do I have to change buses?	**Devo cambiare (autobus)?** _deh_-voh kahm-_byah_-reh (_ow_-toh-boos)
Stop here, please!	**Si fermi qui, per favore!** see _fehr_-mee kwee pehr fah-_voh_-reh

For Tickets, see page 19.

YOU MAY SEE...

FERMATA AUTOBUS	bus stop
ENTRATA/USCITA	enter/exit
CONVALIDA BIGLIETTO	stamp your ticket

When traveling by bus, purchase your ticket before boarding from a tobacconist or from a vending machine at train or subway stations. Tickets have a magnetic strip on the back. Upon boarding the bus, validate your ticket at one of the yellow validation machines on the bus (see picture on page 28). Insert your ticket into the machine with the arrow toward you and pointing downward. The machine will accept the ticket and then return it; a green light shows the ticket is valid and a red light means it is invalid. If the machine does not work, you can try another machine on the bus or write the date, time of day and the bus number on the ticket. If the bus features only the older orange machines, fold the ticket in half lengthwise so that it fits into the machine for validation.

Metro

Where's the metro [underground] station?	**Dov'è la stazione della metropolitana?** *doh·veh lah stah·tsyoh·neh dehl·lah meh·troh·poh·lee·tah·nah*
A map, please.	**Una cartina, per favore.** *oo·nah kahr·tee·nah pehr fah·voh·reh*
Which line for…?	**Che linea devo prendere per…?** *keh lee·neh·ah deh·voh prehn·deh·reh pehr…*
Which direction?	**In quale direzione?** *een kwah·leh dee·reh·tsyoh·neh*

The Italian public transportation system is extensive and generally efficient. Urban areas are served by networks of buses, trams and subways. Tickets are usually sold at **edicole** (newsstands), nearby **caffè** (coffee bars) and **tabacchi** (tobacconists). Discounts are available but vary between locations. Ask the hotel concierge or your travel agent for a schedule.

Do I have to transfer [change]?	**Devo cambiare?** _deh_•voh kahm•_byah_•reh
Is this the subway [train] to…?	**È la metropolitana per…?** eh lah meh•troh•poh•lee•_tah_•nah pehr…
How many stops to…?	**Quante fermate mancano per arrivare a…?** kwahn•teh fehr•mah•teh mahn•kah•noh pehr ahr•ree•vah•reh ah
Where are we?	**Dove siamo?** _doh_•veh _syah_•moh

For Tickets, see page 19.

YOU MAY SEE…

IMBARCAZIONE DI SALVATAGGIO	life boat
GIUBBOTTO DI SALVATAGGIO	life jacket

Boat & Ferry

When is the ferry to…?	**Quando parte il traghetto per…?** _kwahn_•doh _pahr_•teh eel trah•_gheht_•toh pehr…
Can I take my car?	**Posso portare l'auto?** _pohs_•soh pohr•_tah_•reh l•_ow_•toh
What time is the next sailing?	**A che ora è la prossima partenza?** ah keh oh•rah eh lah prohs•see•mah pahr•tehn•tsah
Can I book a seat/cabin?	**Posso prenotare un posto/una cabina?** pohs•soh preh•noh•tah•reh oon poh•stoh/oo•nah kah•bee•nah
How long is the crossing?	**Quanto dura la traversata?** kwahn•toh doo•rah lah trah•vehr•sah•tah

Genova, Livorno, Civitavecchia, Napoli, Messina and Reggio Calabria are the main ferry ports connecting the major and minor Italian islands. Travel along local coastal areas and lakes in Italy is enhanced by an extensive ferry system.

Taxi

Where can I get a taxi?	**Dove posso trovare un taxi?** <u>doh</u>•veh <u>pohs</u>•soh troh•<u>vah</u>•reh oon <u>tah</u>•ksee
Can you send a taxi?	**Posso avere un taxi?** pohs•soh ah•<u>veh</u>•re oon tah•ksee
Do you have the number for a taxi?	**Posso avere un numero per chiamare un taxi?** poh•soh ah•<u>veh</u>•reh oon noo•meh•roh pehr kyah•mah•reh oon tah•ksee
I'd like a taxi now/for tomorrow at (time)...	**Vorrei un taxi subito/domani alle...** vohr•<u>ray</u> oon <u>tah</u>•ksee soo•<u>bee</u>•toh/doh•<u>mah</u>•nee <u>ahl</u>•leh...
Pick me up at (place)...	**Venga a prendermi a...** <u>vehn</u>•gah ah <u>prehn</u>•dehr•mee ah...
I'm going to...	**Vado...** <u>vah</u>•doh...
this address	**a questo indirizzo** ah <u>kweh</u>•stoh een•dee•<u>ree</u>•tsoh
the airport	**all'aeroporto** ahl•lah•eh•roh•<u>pohr</u>•toh
the train [railway] station	**alla stazione ferroviaria** <u>ahl</u>•lah stah•<u>tsyoh</u>•neh fehr•roh•<u>vyah</u>•ryah
I'm late.	**Sono in ritardo.** <u>soh</u>•noh een ree•<u>tahr</u>•doh
Can you drive faster/slower?	**Può andare più velocemente/lentamente?** pwoh ahn•<u>dah</u>•reh pyoo veh•loh•cheh•<u>mehn</u>•teh/ lehn•tah•<u>mehn</u>•teh
Stop/Wait here.	**Si fermi/Mi aspetti qui.** see <u>fehr</u>•mee/ mee ah•<u>speht</u>•tee kwee
How much?	**Quant'è?** kwahn•<u>teh</u>

Get a taxi at taxi stands or reserve by phone; hailing a taxi in the street is not common. Extra charges are added for travel at night (10:00 p.m.–7:00 a.m.), on Sundays and holidays, for extra luggage and for trips outside of town. Tip the driver by rounding off to the nearest euro or two.

You said it	**Aveva detto che erano...** *ah·veh·vah deht·toh*
would cost...	*keh eh·rah·noh...*
Keep the change.	**Tenga il resto.** *tehn·gah eel reh·stoh* →
A receipt, please.	**Una ricevuta, perfavore.** *oo·nah ree·cheh·voo·tah* →
	pehr fah·voh·re

Bicycle & Motorbike

I'd like to hire...	**Vorrei noleggiare...** *vohr·ray noh·leh·djah·reh...*
a bicycle	**una bici** *oo·nah bee·chee*
a moped	**uno scooter** *oo·noh skoo·tehr*
a motorcycle	**una moto** *oo·nah moh·toh*
How much per	**Qual è la tariffa per un giorno/una settimana?**
day/week?	*kwah·leh lah tah·reef·fah pehr oon jyohr·noh/*
	oo·nah seht·tee·mah·nah
Can I have	**Mi può dare un casco/lucchetto?**
a helmet/lock?	*mee pwoh dah·reh oon kah·skoh/look·keht·toh*

Car Hire

Where's the car	**Dov'è un autonoleggio?** *doh·veh oon*
rental [hire]?	*ow·toh·noh·leh·djoh*
I'd like...	**Vorrei...** *vohr·ray...*
a cheap/small car	**un'auto economica/piccola** *oo·now·toh*
	eh·koh·noh·mee·kah/peek·koh·lah
an automatic/	**un'auto con il cambio automatico/manuale**
a manual	*oo·now·toh kohn eel kahm·byoh ow·toh·mah·tee·koh/*
	mah·nwah·leh
air conditioning	**un'auto con l'aria condizionata** *oo·now·toh kohn*
	lah·ryah kohn·dee·tsyoh·nah·tah
a car seat	**un sedile** *oon seh·dee·leh*
How much...?	**Qual è la tariffa...?** *kwah·leh lah tah·reef·fah...*
per day/week	**per un giorno/una settimana** *pehr oon jyohr·noh/*
	oo·nah seht·tee·mah·nah

YOU MAY HEAR…

Ha la patente internazionale? *ah lah pah·tehn·teh een·tehr·nah·tsyoh·nah·leh*
Do you have an international driver's license?

Il passaporto, per favore.
eel pahs·sah·pohr·toh pehr fah·voh·reh
Your passport, please.

Desìdera un'assicurazione supplementare? *deh·zee·deh·rah oo·nah·see·koo·rah·tsyoh·neh soop·pleh·mehn·tah·reh*
Do you want extra insurance?

Deve lasciare un deposito. *deh·veh lah·shah·reh oon deh·poh·zee·toh*
I'll need a deposit.

Metta le iniziali/Firmi qui. *meht·tah leh ee·nee·tsyah·lee/feer·mee kwee*
Initial/Sign here.

per kilometer	**a chilometro** *ah kee·loh·meh·troh*
for unlimited mileage	**con chilometraggio illimitato** *kohn kee·loh·meh·trah·djoh eel·lee·mee·tah·toh*
with insurance	**con l'assicurazione** *kohn l·ahs·see·koo·rah·tsyoh·neh*
Are there discounts?	**Fate sconti?** *fah·teh skohn·tee*

Fuel Station

Where's the fuel station?	**Dov'è un benzinaio?** *doh·veh oon behn·dzee·nah·yoh*
Fill it up.	**Faccia il pieno, per favore.** *fah·chyah eel pyeh·noh pehr fah·voh·reh*
…euros, please.	**…euro, per favore.** …*eh·oo·roh pehr fah·voh·reh*
I'll pay in cash/by credit card.	**Pago in contanti/con carta di credito.** *pah·goh een kohn·tahn·tee/kohn kahr·tah dee kreh·dee·toh*

YOU MAY SEE...

SUPER	super
PREMIUM	premium
DIESEL	diesel

Asking Directions

Is this the way to...?	**Vado bene per...?** _vah·doh beh·neh pehr..._ ✓
How far is it to...?	**Quanto dista...?** _kwahn·toh dees·tah..._ ✓
Where's...?	**Dov'è...?** _doh·veh..._
...Street	**Via...** _vee·ah..._ ✓
this address	**questo indirizzo** _kweh·stoh een·dee·ree·tsoh_ ✓

YOU MAY HEAR...

sempre dritto _sehm·preh dreet·toh_	straight ahead
a sinistra _ah see·nee·strah_	left
a destra _ah deh·strah_	right
all'angolo/dietro l'angolo	on the corner/around
ahl·lahn·goh·loh/dyeh·troh lahn·goh·loh	the corner
di fronte _a dee frohn·teh ah_	opposite
dietro a _dyeh·troh ah_	behind
accanto a _ahk·kahn·toh ah_	next to
dopo _doh·poh_	after
a nord/sud _ah nohrd/sood_	north/south
a est/ovest _ah ehst/oh·vehst_	east/west
al semaforo _ahl seh·mah·foh·roh_	at the traffic light
all'incrocio _ahl·leen·kroh·chyoh_	at the intersection

isolata · block

the highway [motorway]	**l'autostrada** /·ow·toh·<u>strah</u>·dah
Can you show me on the map?	**Può indicarmelo sulla cartina?** ✓ *pwoh een·dee·<u>kahr</u>·meh·loh <u>sool</u>·lah kahr·<u>tee</u>·nah*
I'm lost.	**Mi sono perso m/persa f.** *mee <u>soh</u>·noh pehr·soh/ <u>pehr</u>·sah*

Parking

Can I park here?	**Posso parcheggiare qui?** *pohs·soh pahr·keh·<u>djah</u>·reh kwee*
Where's the parking lot [car park]/ parking meter?	**Dov'è il parcheggio/parchimetro?** *doh·<u>veh</u> eel pahr·<u>keh</u>·djoh/pahr·<u>kee</u>·meh·troh*
How much…?	**Quanto costa…?** *<u>kwahn</u>·toh <u>koh</u>·stah…*
per hour	**all'ora** *ahl·<u>loh</u>·rah*
per day	**al giorno** *ahl <u>jyohr</u>·noh*
for overnight	**per tutta la notte** *pehr <u>toot</u>·tah lah <u>noht</u>·teh*

Breakdown & Repair

My car broke down/ won't start.	**La mia auto ha un'avaria al motore/non parte.** *lah <u>mee</u>·ah <u>ow</u>·toh ah oo·nah·vah·<u>ree</u>·ah ahl moh·<u>toh</u>·reh/nohn <u>pahr</u>·teh*
Can you fix it (today)?	**Può ripararla (oggi)?** *pwoh ree·pah·<u>rahr</u>·lah (<u>oh</u>·djee)*

Street parking in cities in limited; it's best to park in a **parcheggio** (parking lot or garage), day or night. Do not park in areas marked **Divieto di sosta** (no stopping except in emergency), **Divieto di fermata** (no stopping at any time) or **Passo carrabile** (do not block passageway).

YOU MAY SEE…

 STOP — stop

 DARE LA PRECEDENZA — yield

 DIVIETO DI SOSTA — no parking

 CURVA PERICOLOSA — dangerous curve

 SENSO UNICO — one way

 STRADA CHIUSA — road closed

 DIVIETO DI SORPASSO — no passing

 DIVIETO DI INVERSIONE DI MARCIA no u-turn

When will it be ready?	**Per quando è pronta?** *pehr kwahn•doh è prohn•tah*
How much?	**Quanto mi costa?** *kwahn•toh mee koh•stah*
I have a puncture/flat tyre (tire)	**Ho una ruota bucata/sgonfia** *oh oo•nah roo•oh•tah boo•kah•tah/zgohn•fyah*

Accidents

There was an accident.	**C'è stato un incidente.** *cheh stah•toh oon een•chee•dehn•teh*
Call an ambulance/the police.	**Chiami un'ambulanza/la polizia.** *kyah•mee oo•nahm•boo•lahn•tsah/lah poh•lee•tsee•ah*

ESSENTIAL

Can you recommend a hotel?	**Può consigliarmi un hotel?** *pwoh kohn·see·llyahr·mee oon oh·tehl*
I have a reservation.	**Ho una prenotazione.** *oh oo·nah preh·noh·tah·tsyoh·neh*
My name is…	**Mi chiamo…** *mee kyah·moh…*
Do you have a room…?	**Avete una camera…?** *ah·veh·teh oo·nah kah·meh·rah…*
for one/two	**singola/doppia** *seen·goh·lah/dohp·pyah*
with a bathroom	**con bagno** *kohn bah·nyoh*
with air conditioning	**con aria condizionata** *kohn ah·ryah kohn·dee·tsyoh·nah·tah*
For…	**Per…** *pehr…*
tonight	**stanotte** *stah·noht·teh*
two nights	**due notti** *doo·eh noht·tee*
one week	**una settimana** *oo·nah seht·tee·mah·nah*
How much?	**Quanto costa?** *kwahn·toh koh·stah*
Is there anything cheaper?	**C'è qualcosa di più economico?** *cheh kwahl·koh·zah dee pyoo eh·koh·noh·mee·koh*
When's check-out?	**A che ora devo lasciare la camera?** *ah keh oh·rah deh·voh lah·shah·reh lah kah·meh·rah*
Can I leave this in the safe?	**Posso lasciare questo nella cassaforte?** *pohs·soh lah·shah·reh kweh·stoh nehl·lah kahs·sah·fohr·teh*
Can I leave my bags?	**Posso lasciare le valigie?** *pohs·soh lah·shah·reh leh vah·lee·jyeh*
I'd like the bill/receipt.	**Vorrei il conto/la ricevuta.** *vohr·ray eel kohn·toh/lah ree·cheh·voo·tah*

I'll pay in cash/ by credit card.	**Pago in <u>contanti</u>/con carta di credito.** *pah·goh een kohn·<u>tahn</u>·tee/kohn <u>kahr</u>·tah dee <u>kreh</u>·dee·toh*

Somewhere to Stay

Can you recommend...?	**Può consigliarmi...?** *pwoh kohn·see·<u>llyahr</u>·mee...*
a hotel	**un hotel** *oon oh·<u>tehl</u>*
a hostel	**un ostello** *oon oh·<u>stehl</u>·loh*
a campsite	**un campeggio** *oon kahm·<u>peh</u>·djoh*
a bed and breakfast	**una pensione** *<u>oo</u>·nah pehn·<u>syoh</u>·neh*
What is it near?	**Vicino cosa c'è?** *vee·<u>chee</u>·noh <u>koh</u>·zah cheh*
How do I get there?	**Come ci si arriva?** *<u>koh</u>·meh chee see ahr·<u>ree</u>·vah*

At the Hotel

I have a reservation.	**Ho una prenotazione.** *oh <u>oo</u>·nah preh·noh·tah·<u>tsyoh</u>·neh*
My name is...	**Mi chiamo...** *mee <u>kyah</u>·moh...*
Do you have a room...?	**Avete una camera...?** *ah·<u>veh</u>·teh <u>oo</u>·nah <u>kah</u>·meh·rah...*
with a bathroom [toilet]/shower	**con bagno/doccia** *kohn <u>bah</u>·nyoh/ <u>doh</u>·chyah*
with air conditioning	**con aria condizionata** *kohn <u>ah</u>·ryah kohn·dee·tsyoh·<u>nah</u>·tah*
that's smoking/ non-smoking	**per fumatori/non fumatori** *pehr foo·mah·<u>toh</u>·ree/nohn foo·mah·<u>toh</u>·ree*
For...	**Per...** *pehr...*
tonight	**stanotte** *stah·<u>noht</u>·teh*
two nights	**due notti** *<u>doo</u>·eh <u>noht</u>·tee*
a week	**una settimana** *<u>oo</u>·nah seht·tee·<u>mah</u>·nah*

If you didn't reserve accommodations before your trip, visit the local **l'ufficio informazioni turistiche**, tourist information office, for recommendations on places to stay.

Do you have…?	**C'è…?** *cheh…*
a computer	**un computer** *oon kohm·pyoo·tehr*
an elevator [lift]	**l'ascensore** *lah·shehn·soh·reh*
(wireless) internet service	**il collegamento Internet (wireless)** *eel kohl·leh·gah·mehn·toh een·tehr·neht (wyer·lehs)*
room service	**il servizio in camera** *eel sehr·vee·tsyoh een kah·meh·rah*
a pool	**la piscina** *lah pee·shee·nah*
a gym	**la palestra** *lah pah·leh·strah*
I need…	**Mi serve…** *mee sehr·veh…*
an extra bed	**un altro letto** *oon ahl·troh leht·toh*
a cot	**un lettino** *oon leht·tee·noh*
a crib	**una culla** *oo·nah kool·lah*

For Numbers, see page 167.

Price

How much per day/week?	**Quanto costa al giorno/alla settimana?** _kwahn·toh koh·stah ahl jyohr·noh/ahl·lah seht·tee·mah·nah_
Does that include breakfast/sales tax [VAT]?	**La prima colazione/L'IVA è inclusa?** _lah pree·mah koh·lah·tsyoh·neh/lee·vah eh een·kloo·sah_
Are there any discounts?	**Fate sconti?** _fah·teh skohn·tee_

Preferences

Can I see the room?	**Posso vedere la stanza?** _pohs·soh veh·deh·reh lah stahn·tsah_
I'd like a...room.	**Vorrei una...camera.** _vohr·ray oo·nah... kah·meh·rah_
better	**migliore** _mee·llyoh·reh_
bigger	**più grande** _pyoo grahn·deh_
cheaper	**più economica** _pyoo eh·koh·noh·mee·kah_
quieter	**più silenziosa/tranquilla** _pyoo see·lehn·tsyoh·sa/ trahn·kweehl·lah_
I'll take it.	**La prendo.** _lah prehn·doh_
No, I won't take it.	**Non la prendo.** _nohn lah prehn·doh_

A wide variety of accommodation is available in Italy, from budget to luxury. In recent years, **agriturismo** (farm-stays or ecotourism) have become very popular; these offer countryside locations, usually on a working farm, and often serve locally produced food. You may wish to stay in a **villa**, an upscale—and expensive—home or apartment, which often has a pool. **Una pensione** (bed and breakfast) is an ideal accommodation for budget-minded travelers who'd like to experience how Italians live. **Un hotel** can range in quality and price; many international chains have hotels throughout Italy.

YOU MAY HEAR...

Il suo passaporto/La sua carta di credito, per favore. *eel soo•oh pahs•sah•pohr•toh/lah soo•ah kahr•tah dee kreh•dee•toh pehr fah•voh•reh*	Your passport/credit card, please.
Compili questo modulo. *kohm•pee•lee kweh•stoh moh•doo•loh*	Fill out this form.
Firmi qui. *feer•mee kwee*	Sign here.

Questions

Where's...?	**Dov'è...?** *doh•veh...*
the bar	**il bar** *eel bahr*
the toilet	**la toilette** *lah twah•leht*
the elevator [lift]	**l'ascensore** *lah•shehn•soh•reh*
Can I have...?	**Può darmi...?** *pwoh dahr•mee...*
a blanket	**una coperta** *oo•nah koh•pehr•tah*
an iron	**un ferro da stiro** *oon fehr•roh dah stee•roh*
a pillow	**un cuscino** *oon koo•shee•noh*
soap	**una saponetta** *oo•nah sah•poh•neht•tah*
the room key/ key card	**la chiave/la chiave magnetica della camera** *lah kyah•veh/lah kyah•veh mah•nyeh•tee•kah dehl•lah kah•meh•rah*
toilet paper	**della carta igienica** *dehl•lah kahr•tah ee•jyeh•nee•kah*
a towel	**un asciugamano** *oon ah•shoo•gah•mah•noh*
Do you have an adapter for this?	**Avete un adattatore?** *ah•veh•teh oon ah•daht•toh•tohr•eh*
How do I turn on the lights?	**Come si accendono le luci?** *koh•meh see ah•chehn•doh•noh leh loo•chee*
Can you wake me at...?	**Può svegliarmi alle...?** *pwoh zveh•llyahr•mee ahl•leh...*

Can I leave this in the safe?	**Posso lasciare questo nella cassaforte?** _pohs•soh lah•shah•reh kweh•stoh nehl•lah kahs•sah•fohr•teh_
Can I have my things from the safe?	**Posso prendere le mie cose dalla cassaforte?** _pohs•soh prehn•deh•reh leh mee•eh koh•zeh dahl•lah kahs•sah•fohr•teh_
Is there mail [post]/ a message for me?	**C'è posta/Ci sono messaggi per me?** _cheh poh•stah/chee soh•noh mehs•sah•djee pehr meh_
Do you have a laundry service?	**Fate servizio di lavanderia?** _Fah•teh sehr•vee•tsyohdee lah•vahn•deh•ree•ah_

Problems

There's a problem.	**C'è un problema.** _cheh oon proh•bleh•mah_
I lost my key/key card.	**Ho perso la chiave/chiave elettronica.** _oh pehr•soh lah kyah•veh/kyah•veh eh•leht•troh•nee•kah_
I'm locked out of the room.	**Sono rimasto chiuso?/rimasta chiusa/fuori.** _soh•noh ree•mah•stoh kyoo•zoh?/ree•mah•stah kyoo•zah/fwoh•ree_
There's no hot water/toilet paper.	**Non c'è acqua calda/carta igienica.** _nohn cheh ah•kwah kahl•dah/kahr•tah ee•jyeh•nee•kah_
The room is dirty.	**La camera è sporca.** _lah kah•meh•rah eh spohr•kah_
There are bugs in the room.	**In camera ci sono degli insetti.** _een kah•meh•rah chee soh•noh deh•llyee een•seht•tee_
The…doesn't work.	**…non funziona.** _…nohn foon•tsyoh•nah_
Can you fix…?	**Può riparare…?** _pwoh ree•pah•rah•reh…_
the air conditioning	**l'aria condizionata** _lah•ryah kohn•dee•tsyoh•nah•tah_
the fan	**il ventilatore** _eel vehn•tee•lah•toh•reh_
the heat [heating]	**il riscaldamento** _eel ree•skahl•dah•mehn•toh_
the light	**la luce** _lah loo•cheh_
the TV	**la TV** _lah tee•voo_
the toilet	**il gabinetto** _eel gah•bee•neht•toh_
I'd like another room.	**Vorrei un'altra camera.** _vohr•ray oo•nahl•trah kah•meh•rah_

YOU MAY SEE...

SPINGERE/TIRARE	push/pull
TOILETTE	bathroom [toilet]
DOCCIA	shower
ASCENSORE	elevator [lift]
SCALE	stairs
LAVANDERIA	laundry
NON DISTURBARE	do not disturb
PORTA ANTINCENDIO	fire door
USCITA (D'EMERGENZA)	(emergency) exit
SERVIZIO SVEGLIA	wake-up call

Checking Out

When's check-out?	**A che ora devo lasciare la camera?** *ah keh oh•rah deh•voh lah•shah•reh lah kah•meh•rah*
Can I leave my bags here until...?	**Posso lasciare le valigie fino alle...?** *pohs•soh lah•shah•reh leh vah•lee•jyeh fee•noh ahl•leh...*
Can I have an itemized bill/receipt?	**Posso avere il conto dettagliato/la ricevuta?** *pohs•soh ah•veh•reh eel kohn•toh deht•tah•llyah•toh/ lah ree•cheh•voo•tah*
I think there's a mistake.	**Credo che ci sia un errore.** *kreh•doh keh chee see•ah oon ehr•roh•reh*
I'll pay in cash/by credit card.	**Pago in contanti/con carta di credito.** *pah•ghoh een kohn•tahn•tee/kohn kahr•tah dee kreh•dee•toh*

Voltage is 220–240V, and plugs are two-pronged. You may need a converter and/or an adapter for your appliances.

A service fee is generally included in bills throughout Italy. It's optional to tip porters and housekeeping staff, though a tip for good service is always appreciated. Your concierge will appreciate a tip for any helpful services provided.

Renting

I reserved an apartment/a room.	**Ho prenotato un appartamento/una camera.** *oh preh·noh·tah·toh oon ahp·pahr·tah·mehn·toh/ oo·nah kah·meh·rah*
My name is…	**Mi chiamo…** *mee kyah·moh…*
Can I have the key/key card?	**Mi può dare la chiave/chiave elettronica?** *mee pwoo dah·reh lah kyah·veh/kyah·veh eh·leht·troh·nee·kah*
Are there…?	**Ci sono…?** *chee soh·noh…*
dishes	**i piatti** *ee pyaht·tee*
pillows	**i cuscini** *ee koo·shee·nee*
sheets	**le lenzuola** *leh lehn·tswoh·lah*
towels	**gli asciugamani** *llyee ah·shoo·gah·mah·nee*
kitchen utensils	**gli utensili** *llyee oo·tehn·see·lee*
When do I put out the bins/ recycling?	**Quando si mette fuori il secchio della spazzatura/il riciclaggio?** *kwahn·doh see meht·teh fwoh·ree eel sehk·kyoh dehl·lah spah·tsah·too·rah/ eel ree·chee·klah·djoh*
…is broken.	**…non funziona.** *…nohn foon·tsyoh·nah*
How does…work?	**Come funziona…?** *koh·meh foon·tsyoh·nah…*
the air conditioner	**il condizionatore** *eel kohn·dee·tsyoh·nah·toh·reh*
the dishwasher	**la lavastoviglie** *lah lah·vah·stoh·vee·llyeh*
the freezer	**il freezer** *eel free·zehr*
the heater	**il riscaldamento** *eel ree·skahl·dah·mehn·toh*
the microwave	**il microonde** *eel mee·kroh·ohn·deh*

the refrigerator	**il frigo** *eel free·goh*
the stove	**la cucina** *lah koo·chee·nah*
the washing machine	**la lavatrice** *lah lah·vah·tree·cheh*

Domestic Items

I need...	**Ho bisogno di...** *oh bee·soh·nyoh dee...*
an adapter	**un adattatore** *oon ah·daht·toh·toh·reh*
aluminum [kitchen] foil	**carta stagnola** *kahr·tah stah·nyoh·lah*
a bottle opener	**un apribottiglie** *oon ah·pree·boht·tee·llyeh*
a broom	**una scopa** *oo·nah skoh·pah*
a can opener	**un apriscatole** *oon ah·pree·skah·toh·leh*
cleaning supplies	**prodotti per le pulizie** *proh·doht·tee pehr leh poo·lee·tsee·eh*
a corkscrew	**un cavatappi** *oon kah·vah·tahp·pee*
detergent	**detersivo** *deh·tehr·see·voh*
dishwashing liquid	**detersivo per i piatti** *deh·tehr·see·voh pehr ee pyaht·tee*
bin bags	**sacchetti per i rifiuti** *sahk·keht·tee pehr ee ree·fyoo·tee*
a lightbulb	**una lampadina** *oo·nah lahm·pah·dee·nah*
matches	**fiammiferi** *fyahm·mee·feh·ree*

a mop	**un mocio** *oon <u>moh</u>•choh*
napkins	**tovaglioli** *toh•vah•<u>llyoh</u>•lee*
paper towels	**carta da cucina** *<u>kahr</u>•tah dah koo•<u>chee</u>•nah*
plastic wrap	**pellicola per alimenti** *pehl•<u>lee</u>•koh•lah*
[cling film]	*pehr ah•lee•<u>mehn</u>•tee*
a plunger	**uno sturalavandini** *<u>oo</u>•noh stoo•rah•lah•vahn•<u>dee</u>•nee*
scissors	**un paio di forbici** *oon <u>pah</u>•yoh dee <u>fohr</u>•bee•chee*
a vacuum cleaner	**un aspirapolvere** *oon ah•spee•rah•<u>pohl</u>•veh•reh*

For In the Kitchen, see page 78.

For Conversion Tables, see page 172.

At the Hostel

Is there a bed available?	**C'è un letto disponibile?** *cheh oon <u>leht</u>•toh dee•spoh•<u>nee</u>•bee•leh*
Can I have...?	**Potrei avere...?** *poh•<u>tray</u> ah•<u>veh</u>•reh*
a single/double room	**una camera singola/doppia** *<u>oo</u>•nah <u>kah</u>•meh•rah <u>seen</u>•goh•lah/<u>dohp</u>•pyah*
a blanket	**una coperta** *<u>oo</u>•nah koh•<u>pehr</u>•tah*
a pillow	**un cuscino** *oon koo•<u>shee</u>•noh*
sheets	**delle lenzuola** *<u>dehl</u>•leh lehn•<u>tswoh</u>•lah*
a towel	**un asciugamano** *oon ah•shoo•gah•<u>mah</u>•noh*

Hostels are inexpensive accommodations that have dormitory-style sleeping arrangements and private or semi-private rooms. Some hostels have rooms with private bathrooms, though most offer shared bathrooms. There is usually a self-service kitchen on site. Reservations are recommended in advance in larger cities and popular tourist destinations during the tourist season. Visit the Hosteling International website for details.

Do you have lockers?	**Avete gli armadietti col lucchetto?** *ah·veh·the llyee ahr·mah·dyeht·tee khol look·keht·toh*
When do you lock up?	**A che ora chiudete?** *ah keh oh·rah kyoo·deh·teh*
Do I need a membership card?	**Ci vuole la tessera di iscrizione?** *chee vwoh·leh lah teh·seh·rah deehs·kree·tsyoh·neh*
Here's my international student card.	**Ecco la mia tessera studentesca internazionale.** *ehk·koh lah mee·ah teh·seh·rah stoo·dehn·tehs·kah een·tehr·nah·tsyoh·nah·leh*

Going Camping

Can I camp here?	**Si può campeggiare?** *see pwoh kahm·peh·djah·reh*
Where's the campsite?	**Dov'è il campeggio?** *doh·veh eel kahm·peh·djoh*
What is the charge per day/week?	**Qual è la tariffa per un giorno/una settimana?** *kwah·leh lah tah·reef·fah pehr oon jyohr·noh/ oo·nah seht·tee·mah·nah*
Are there...?	**Ci sono...?** *chee soh·noh...*
cooking facilities	**le attrezzature per cucinare** *leh aht·treh·tsah·too·reh pehr koo·chee·nah·reh*
electric outlets	**le prese elettriche** *leh preh·seh eh·leht·tree·keh*
laundry facilities	**le lavanderie** *leh lah·vahn·deh·ree·eh*
showers	**le docce** *leh doh·cheh*
tents for rent [hire]	**tende a noleggio** *tehn·deh ah noh·leh·djoh*

YOU MAY SEE...

ACQUA POTABILE	drinking water
NO CAMPING	no camping
DIVIETO DI FALÒ/BARBECUE	no fires/barbecues

Where can I empty the chemical toilet?	**Dove posso vuotare il water?** *doh•veh pohs•soh vwoh•tah•reh eel vah•tehr*

For Domestic Items, see page 44.

For In the Kitchen, see page 78.

Communications

ESSENTIAL

Where's an internet cafe?	**Dov'è un Internet caffè?** *doh•veh oon een•tehr•neht kahf•feh*
Can I access the internet/check e-mail?	**Posso collegarmi a Internet/controllare le e-mail?** *pohs•soh kohl•leh•gahr•mee ah een•tehr•neht/kohn•trohl•lah•reh leh ee•mayl*
How much per hour/half hour?	**Quanto costa per un'ora/mezz'ora?** *kwahn•toh koh•stah pehr oon•oh•rah/mehdz•oh•rah*
How do I log on?	**Come si fa il login?** *koh•meh see fah eel loh•geen*
A phone card, please.	**Una scheda telefonica, per favore.** *oo•nah skeh•dah teh•leh•foh•nee•kah pehr fah•voh•reh*
Can I have your number, please?	**Mi può dare il suo numero, per favore?** *mee pwoh dah•reh eel soo•oh noo•meh•roh pehr fah•voh•reh*
Here's my number/e-mail.	**Ecco il mio numero/la mia e-mail.** *ehk•koh eel mee•oh noo•meh•roh/lah mee•ah ee•mayl*
Call/E-mail me.	**Mi chiami/mandi una e-mail.** *mee kyah•mee/mahn•dee oo•nah ee•mayl*
Hello. This is...	**Pronto. Sono...** *prohn•toh soh•noh...*
Can I speak to...?	**Posso parlare con...?** *pohs•soh pahr•lah•reh kohn...*
Can you repeat that?	**Può ripetere?** *pwoh ree•peh•teh•reh*
I'll call back later.	**Richiamo più tardi.** *ree•kyah•moh pyoo tahr•dee*

Bye.	**Arrivederla.** ahr·ree·veh·dehr·lah
Where's the post office?	**Dov'è un ufficio postale?** doh·veh oon oof·fee·chyoh poh·stah·leh
I'd like to send this to...	**Vorrei inviare questo a...** vohr·ray een·vyah·reh kweh·stoh ah...

Online

Where's an internet cafe?	**Dov'è un Internet caffè?** doh·veh oon een·tehr·neht kahf·feh
Does it have wireless internet?	**C'è il wireless?** cheh eel wyehr·lehs
What is the WiFi password?	**Qual è la password Wi-Fi?** koo·ahl·eh lah pahs·swoh·rd wah·ee fah·ee
Is the WiFi free?	**Il WiFi è gratis?** Eel wah·ee fah·ee eh grah·tees
Do you have bluetooth?	**Avete il Bluetooth?** Ah·veh·teh eel bloo·too·th
How do I turn the computer on/off?	**Come si accende/spegne il computer?** koh·meh see ah·chehn·deh/speh·nyeh eel kohm·pyoo·tehr
Can I...?	**Posso...?** pohs·soh...
access the internet	**collegarmi (a Internet)** kohl·leh·gahr·mee (ah een·tehr·neht)
check e-mail	**controllare le e-mail** kohn·trohl·lah·reh leh ee·mayl
print	**stampare** stahm·pah·reh
plug in/charge my laptop/iPhone/iPad/BlackBerry?	**collegare/ricaricare il mio portatile/iPhone/iPad?** kohl·leh·gah·reh eel mee·oh pohr·tah·tee·leh/ahy·fon/ahy·pad
access Skype?	**usare Skype?** oo·sah·reh skah·eep

How much per hour/half hour?	**Quanto costa per un'ora/mezz'ora?** *kwahn•toh koh•stah pehr oon•oh•rah/mehdz•oh•rah*	
How do I...?	**Come...?** *koh•meh...*	
connect/ disconnect	**ci si collega/scollega** *chee see kohl•leh•gah/ skohl•leh•gah*	
log on/log off	**si fa il login/logout** *see fah eel loh•geen/loh•gowt*	
type this symbol	**digiti questo simbolo** *dee•jee•tee kweh•stoh seem•boh•loh*	
What's your e-mail?	**Qual è la sua e-mail?** *kwahl•eh lah soo•ah ee•mayl*	
My e-mail is...	**La mia e-mail è...** *lah mee•ah ee•mayl eh...*	
Do you have a scanner?	**Avete uno scanner?** *ah•veh•teh oo•noh skahn•nehr*	

Social Media

Are you on Facebook/ Twitter?	**È su Facebook/Twitter?** *(polite form)* *eh soo feh•eez•book/tweet•tehr*
	Sei su Facebook/Twitter? *(informal form)* *seh•ee soo feh•eez•book/tweet•tehr*
What's your user name?	**Qual è il suo nome utente?** *(polite form)* *koo•ahl eh eel soo•oh noh•meh oo•tehn•teh*
	Qual è il tuo nome utente? *(informal form)* *Koo•ahl•eh eel too•oh noh•meh oo•tehn•teh*

I'll add you as a friend. **La aggiungerò come amico.** *(polite form)*
lah ah•djoon•djeh•roh koh•meh ah•mee•koh

Ti aggiungerò come amico. *(informal form)*
tee ah•djoon•djeh•roh koh•meh ah•mee•koh

I'll follow you Twitter. **La seguirò su Twitter.** *(polite form)* *lah seh•gwee•roh soo tweet•tehr*

Ti seguirò su Twitter. *(informal form)* *tee seh•gwee•roh soo tweet•tehr*

Are you following...? **Segue...?** *(polite form)* *seh•gweh...*

Seguite...? *(informal form)* *seh•gwee•teh...*

I'll put the pictures on **Metterò le foto su Facebook/Twitter.**

YOU MAY SEE...

CHIUDI	close
ELIMINA	delete
E-MAIL	e-mail
ESCI	exit
AIUTO	help
INSTANT MESSENGER	instant messenger
INTERNET	internet
LOGIN	login
NUOVO (MESSAGGIO)	new (message)
ACCESSO/SPENTO	on/off
APRI	open
STAMPA	print
SALVA	save
INVIA	send
NOME UTENTE/PASSWORD	username/password
WIRELESS	wireless internet

meht·teh·roh leh foh·toh soo feh·eez·book/tweet·tehr
La taggherò nelle foto. *(polite form)*
lah tahg·gheh·roh nehl·leh foh·toh
Ti taggherò nelle foto. *(informal form)*
tee tahg·gheh·roh nehl·leh foh·toh

Phone

A phone card/
prepaid phone please.

**Una scheda telefonica/ telefonoprepagato,
per favore.** *oo·nah skeh·dah teh·leh·foh·nee·kah/
teh·leh·foh·noh preh·pah·gah·toh pehr fah·voh·reh*

How much? **Quant'è?** *kwahn·teh*

Where's the
pay phone?

**Dove posso trovare un telefono pubblico/
una cabina telefonica?** *doh·veh pohs·soh
troh·vah·reh oon teh·leh·foh·noh puhb·blee·koh/
oo·nah kah·bee·nah teh·leh·foh·nee·kah*

What's the area
code/country
code for...?

Qual è il prefisso/prefisso internazionale per...?
*kwahl eh eel preh·fees·soh/preh·fees·soh
een·tehr·nah·tsyoh·nah·leh pehr...*

What's the number
for Information?

Che numero ha il servizio informazioni?
*keh noo·meh·roh ah eel sehr·vee·tsyoh
een·fohr·mah·tsyoh·nee*

I'd like the
number for...

Vorrei il numero di/del/della/dell'...
vohr·ray eel noo·meh·roh pehr dee/dehl/dehl·lah/dehl...

I'd like to call collect
[reverse the charges].

**Vorrei fare una telefonata a carico del
destinatario.** *vohr·ray fah·reh oo·nah
teh·leh·foh·nah·tah ah kah·ree·koh dehl
deh·stee·nah·tah·ryoh*

My phone doesn't
work here.

Il telefonino non prende. *eel teh·leh·foh·nee·noh
nohn prehn·deh*

What network are
you on?

Su quale rete siamo? *soo koo·ah·leh reh·teh
syah·moh*

Is it 3G?	**È una rete 3G?** *eh oo•nah reh•teh treh djee*
I have run out of credit/minutes.	**Non ho più credito/minuti.** *nohn oh pyoo kreh•dee•toh/mee•noo•tee*
Can I buy some credit?	**Posso acquistare una ricarica?** *pohs•soh ah•kwee•stah•reh oo•nah ree•kah•ree•kah*
Do you have a phone charger?	**Avete un caricabatterie per il telefono?** *Ah•veh•teh oon kah•ree•kah•baht•teh•ree•eh pehr eel teh•leh•foh•noh*
Can I have your number, please?	**Mi può dare il suo numero, per favore?** *mee pwoh dah•reh eel soo•oh noo•meh•roh pehr fah•voh•reh*

YOU MAY HEAR...

Chi parla? *kee pahr•lah*	Who's calling?
Attenda. *aht•tehn•dah*	Hold on.
Le passo il numero. *leh pahs•soh eel noo•meh•roh*	I'll put you through.
Non c'è. *nohn cheh*	He/She is not here.
È al telefono. *eh ahl teh•leh•foh•noh*	He/She is on another line.
Vuole lasciare un messaggio? *vwoh•leh lah•shah•reh oon mehs•sah•djoh*	Would you like to leave a message?
Richiami più tardi/fra dieci minuti. *ree•kyah•mee pyoo tahr•dee/frah dyeh•chee mee•noo•tee*	Call back later/in 10 minutes.
Può richiamarla? *pwoh ree•kyah•mahr•lah*	Can he/she call you back?
Mi lascia il suo numero? *mee lah•shah eel soo•oh noo•meh•roh*	What's your number?

Most public phones are card-operated; phone cards can be purchased at **edicole** (newsstands), **caffè** (coffee bars) and **tabacchi** (tobacconists). For international calls, calling cards are the most economical. Calling internationally from your hotel may be convenient, but the rates can be very expensive.

To call the U.S. or Canada from Italy, dial 001 + area code + phone number. To call the U.K. from Italy, dial 0044 + area code (minus the first 0) + phone number.

To make a local or national call within Italy, dial the area code then the phone number. A list of codes can be found in the phone book.

Here's my number.	**Ecco il mio numero.** _ehk_·koh eel _mee_·oh _noo_·meh·roh
Call/Text me.	**Mi chiami/mandi un SMS.** mee _kyah_·mee/ _mahn_·dee oon _ehs_·seh _ehm_·meh _ehs_·seh
I'll call you.	**La chiamo.** lah _kyah_·moh
I'll text you.	**Le mando un SMS.** leh _mahn_·doh oon _ehs_·seh _ehm_·meh _ehs_·seh

For Grammar, see page 162.

For Numbers, see page 167.

Telephone Etiquette

Hello. This is…	**Pronto. Sono…** _prohn_·toh _soh_·noh…
Can I speak to…?	**Posso parlare con…?** _pohs_·soh pahr·_lah_·reh kohn…
Extension…	**Interno…** een·_tehr_·noh…
Speak louder/more slowly, please.	**Parli più forte/lentamente, per favore.** _pahr_·lee pyoo _fohr_·teh/lehn·tah·_mehn_·teh pehr fah·_voh_·reh

Gli uffici postali (post offices) are open Monday through Friday 8:30 a.m. to 6:30 p.m. and Saturday from 8:30 a.m. to 12:30 p.m. If you need to send valuable items, choose **posta raccomandata** (registered mail). Stamps can also be purchased at **tabacchi** (tobacconists).

Can you repeat that?	**Può ripetere?** *pwoh ree•peh•teh•reh*
I'll call back later.	**Richiamo più tardi.** *ree•kyah•moh pyoo tahr•dee*
Bye.	**Arrivederla.** *ahr•ree•veh•dehr•lah*

For Business Travel, see page 141.

Fax

Can I send/receive a fax here?	**Posso inviare/ricevere un fax?** *pohs•soh een•vyah•reh/ree•cheh•veh•reh oon fahks*
What's the fax number?	**Qual è il numero di fax?** *kwahl•eh eel noo•meh•roh dee fahks*
Please fax this to…	**Invii questo fax a…, per favore.** *een•vee•ee kweh•stoh fahks ah…pehr fah•voh•reh*

YOU MAY HEAR…

Riempia il modulo per la dogana. *ryehm•pee•ah eel moh•doo•loh pehr lah doh•gah•nah*	Fill out the customs declaration form.
Valore? *vah•loh•reh*	What's the value?
Cosa c'è dentro? *koh•zah cheh dehn•troh*	What's inside?

Post

Where's the post office/mailbox [postbox]?	**Dov'è un ufficio postale/una buca delle lettere?** *doh·veh oon oof·fee·chyoh poh·stah·leh/oo·nah boo·kah dehl·leh leht·teh·reh*
A stamp for this postcard/letter to...	**Un francobollo per questa cartolina/ lettera per...** *oon frahn·koh·bohl·loh pehr kweh·stah kahr·toh·lee·nah/leht·teh·rah pehr...*
How much?	**Quant'è?** *kwahn·teh*
Send this package by airmail/express.	**Mandi questo pacco per posta aerea/ espresso.** *mahn·dee kweh·stoh pahk·koh pehr poh·stah ah·eh·reh·ah/eh·sprehs·soh*
A receipt, please.	**La ricevuta, per favore.** *lah ree·cheh·voo·tah pehr fah·voh·reh*

Food & Drink

ESSENTIAL

Can you recommend a good restaurant/ bar?	**Può consigliarmi un buon ristorante/bar?** *pwoh kohn•see•llyahr•mee oon bwohn ree•stoh•rahn•teh/bahr*
Is there a traditional/ an inexpensive restaurant nearby?	**C'è un ristorante tipico/economico qui vicino?** *cheh oon ree•stoh•rahn•teh tee•pee•koh/ eh•koh•noh•mee•koh kwee vee•chee•noh*
A table for…, please.	**Un tavolo per…, per favore.** *oon tah•voh•loh pehr… pehr fah•voh•reh*
Can we sit…?	**Possiamo sederci…?** *pohs•syah•moh seh•dehr•chee…*
here/there	**qui/là** *kwee/lah*
outside	**fuori** *fwoh•ree*
in a (non-) smoking area	**in una sala per (non) fumatori** *een oo•nah sah•lah pehr (nohn) foo•mah•toh•ree*
I'm waiting for someone.	**Sto aspettando qualcuno.** *stoh ah•speht•tahn•doh kwahl•koo•noh*
Where are the toilets?	**Dov'è la toilette?** *doh•veh lah twah•leht*
The menu, please.	**Il menù, per favore.** *eel meh•noo pehr fah•voh•reh*
What do you recommend?	**Cosa mi consiglia?** *koh•zah mee kohn•see•llyah*
I'd like…	**Vorrei…** *vohr•ray…*
Some more …, please.	**Un po' di più…, per favore** *oon poh dee pyoo, pehr fah•voh•reh*
Enjoy your meal!	**Buon appetito!** *bwohn ahp•peh•tee•toh*
The check [bill], please.	**Il conto, per favore.** *eel kohn•toh pehr fah•voh•reh*

Is service included?	**Il servizio è compreso?** *eel sehr•vee•tsyoh* ✓ *eh kohm•preh•zoh*
Can I pay by credit card/have a receipt?	**Posso pagare con carta di credito/avere una ricevuta?** *pohs•soh pah•gah•reh kohn kahr•tah dee kreh•dee•toh/ah•veh•reh oo•nah ree•cheh•voo•tah*
Thank you!	**Grazie!** *grah•tsyeh*

Where to Eat

Can you recommend...?	**Può consigliarmi...?** *pwoh kohn•see•llyahr•mee...*
a restaurant	**un ristorante** *oon ree•stoh•rahn•teh*
a bar	**un bar** *oon bahr*
a cafe	**un caffè** *oon kahf•feh*
a fast-food place	**un fast food** *oon fahst food*
a cheap restaurant	**un ristorante economico** *oon ree•stoh•rahn•teh eh•koh•noh•mee•koh*
an expensive restaurant	**un ristorante costoso/caro** *oon ree•stoh•rahn•teh kohs•toh•zoh/kah•roh*
a restaurant with a good view	**un ristorante con una bella vista/un bel panorama** *oon ree•stoh•rahn•teh kohn oo•nah behl•lah vees•tah/oon behl pah•noh•rah•mah*
an authentic/ a non-touristy restaurant	**un ristorante tradizionale/non turistico** *oon ree•stoh•rahn•teh trah•dee•tsyoh•nah•leh/ nohn too•rees•tee•koh*

Reservations & Preferences

We have a reservation.	**Abbiamo prenotato.** *ahb•byah•moh preh•noh•tah•toh*
My name is...	**Mi chiamo...** *mee kyah•moh...*

I'd like to reserve a table…	**Vorrei prenotare un tavolo…** vohr·_ray_ preh·noh·_tah_·reh oon _tah_·voh·loh…
for two	**per due** pehr _doo_·eh
for this evening	**per questa sera** pehr _kweh_·stah _seh_·rah
for tomorrow at…	**per domani alle…** pehr doh·_mah_·nee _ahl_·leh…
A table for two, please.	**Un tavolo per due, per favore.** oon _tah_·voh·loh pehr _doo_·eh pehr fah·_voh_·reh
Can we sit…?	**Possiamo sederci…** pohs·_syah_·moh seh·_dehr_·chee…
here/there	**qui/là** kwee/lah
outside	**fuori** _fwoh_·ree
in a (non-) smoking area	**in una sala per (non) fumatori** een _oo_·nah _sah_·lah pehr (nohn) foo·mah·_toh_·ree

---

La prima colazione (breakfast) is typically espresso or cappuccino with a croissant or sweet pastry. **Il pranzo** (lunch) is served between 12:00 p.m. and 2:00 p.m. and is usually the main meal of the day. **La cena** (dinner) is served between 7:00 p.m. and 10:00 p.m. **Le merende** (snacks) are popular at mid-morning or mid-afternoon; these include a sweet pastry, ice cream or small pizza.

YOU MAY HEAR…

Ha prenotato?	Do you have
ah preh·noh·tah·toh	a reservation?
Per quante persone?	How many?
pehr kwahn·teh pehr·soh·neh	
✓ **Volete ordinare?**	Are you ready
to voh·leh·teh ohr·dee·nah·reh	order?
✓ **Che cosa desidera?**	What would you like?
keh koh·zah deh·zee·deh·rah	
Le consiglio… *leh kohn·see·llyoh…*	I recommend…
Buon appetito. *bwohn ahp·peh·tee·toh*	Enjoy your meal.

by the window	✓ **vicino alla finestra**	*vee·chee·noh ahl·lah fee·neh·strah*
in the shade	✓ **all'ombra**	*ahl·lohm·brah*
in the sun	**al sole**	*ahl soh·leh*
Where are	**Dov'è la toilette?**	
the toilets?	*doh·veh lah twah·leht*	

How to Order

Excuse me!	✓ **Scusi!** *skooh·see*
We're ready	✓ **Vorremmo ordinare.** *vohr·rehm·moh*
to order.	*ohr·dee·nah·reh*
May I see the	**La carta dei vini, per favore.** *lah kahr·tah day*
wine list?	*vee·nee pehr fah·voh·reh*
I'd like…	**Vorrei…** *vohr·ray…*
a bottle of…	**una bottiglia di…** *oo·nah boht·tee·llyah dee…*
a carafe of…	**una caraffa di…** *oo·nah kah·rahf·fah dee…*
a glass of…	**un bicchiere di…** *oon beek·kyeh·reh dee…*
Can I have a menu?	**Il menù, per favore.** *eel meh·noo pehr fah·voh·reh*

Do you have…?	**Avete…?** ah·<u>veh</u>·teh…
a menu in English	**un menù in inglese** oon meh·<u>noo</u> een een·<u>gleh</u>·zeh
a fixed-price menu	**un menù a prezzo fisso** oon meh·<u>noo</u> ah <u>preh</u>·tsoh <u>fees</u>·soh
a children's menu	**un menù per bambini** oon meh·<u>noo</u> pehr bahm·<u>bee</u>·nee
What do you recommend?	**Cosa mi consiglia?** <u>koh</u>·zah mee kohn·<u>see</u>·llyah
What's this?	**Questo che cos'è?** <u>kweh</u>·stoh keh koh·<u>zeh</u>
What's in it?	**Cosa c'è dentro?** <u>koh</u>·zah cheh <u>dehn</u>·troh
Is it spicy?	**È piccante?** eh peek·<u>kahn</u>·the
I'd like…	**Vorrei…** vohr·ray…
More…	**Dell'altro m /altra f …** dehl·lahl·troh/lahl·trah…
With/Without…	**Con/Senza…** kohn/sehn·tsah…
I can't have…	**Non posso mangiare…** nohn pohs·soh mahn·jyah·reh…
rare	**al sangue** ahl sahn·gweh
medium	**mediamente cotta** meh·dyah·mehn·teh koht·tah
well-done	**ben cotta** behn koht·tah
It's to go [take away].	**È da portare via.** eh dah pohr·<u>tahr</u>·eh <u>vee</u>·ah

For Drinks, see page 80.

YOU MAY SEE…

COPERTO	cover charge
PREZZO FISSO	fixed-price
MENÙ	menu
MENÙ DEL GIORNO	menu of the day
SERVIZIO (NON) COMPRESO	service (not) included
SPECIALITÀ DEL GIORNO	daily specials

Cooking Methods

baked	✓	**al forno** *ahl fohr-noh*
boiled		**lesso** *lehs-soh*
braised	✓	**brasato** *brah-zah-toh*
breaded	✓	**impanato** *eem-pah-nah-toh*
creamed		**passato** *pahs-sah-toh*
diced		**a cubetti** *ah koo-beht-tee*
filleted		**filetto** *fee-leht-toh*
fried		**fritto** *freet-toh*
grilled		**grigliato** *gree-llyah-toh*
poached		**in bianco** *een byahn-koh*
roasted		**arrosto** *ahr-roh-stoh*
sautéed		**saltato** *sahl-tah-toh*
smoked	✓	**affumicato** *ahf-foo-mee-kah-toh*
steamed		**al vapore** *ahl vah-poh-reh*
stewed		**stufato** *stoo-fah-toh*
stuffed	✓	**ripieno** *ree-pyeh-noh*

Dietary Requirements

I'm…	**Sono…** *soh-noh…*
diabetic	**diabetico** m /**diabetica** f *dyah-beh-tee-koh/ dyah-beh-tee-kah*
lactose intolerant	**intollerante al lattosio** *een-tohl-leh-rahn-the ahl laht-toh-syoh*
vegetarian	**vegetariano** m /**vegetariana** f *veh-jeh-tah-ryah-noh/veh-jeh-tah-ryah-nah*
vegan	**vegano** m /**vegana** f *veh-gah-noh/veh-gah-nah*
I'm allergic to…	**Sono allergico** m /**allergica** f **a…** *soh-noh ahl-lehr-jee-koh/ahl-lehr-jee-kah ah…*
I can't eat…	**Non posso mangiare…** *nohn pohs-soh mahn-jyah-reh…*
dairy products	**i latticini** *ee laht-tee-chee-nee*

gluten	**il glutine** *eel gloo·tee·neh*	
nuts	**le noci** *leh noh·chee*	
pork	**il maiale** *eel mah·yah·leh*	
shellfish	**i frutti di mare** *ee froot·tee dee mah·reh*	
spicy foods	**i cibi piccanti** *ee chee·bee peek·kahn·tee*	
wheat	**il grano** *eel grah·noh*	
Is it kosher?	**È kosher?** *eh koh·shehr*	
Do you have...?	**Avete...?** *Ah·veh·teh*	
skimmed milk	**latte scremato** *laht·teh skreh·mah·toh*	
whole milk	**latte intero** *laht·teh een·teh·roh*	
soya milk	**latte di soia** *laht·teh dee soh·jah*	

Dining with Children

Do you have children's portions?	**Ci sono porzioni per bambini?** *chee soh·noh pohr·tsyoh·nee pehr bahm·bee·nee*
Can I have a highchair/child's seat?	**Un seggiolone/seggiolino da bambino, per favore.** *oon seh·djoh·loh·neh/seh·djoh·lee·noh dah bahm·bee·noh pehr fah·voh·reh*
Where can I feed/ change the baby?	**Dove posso dare da mangiare al/cambiare il bambino?** *doh·veh pohs·soh dah·reh dah mahn·jyah·reh ahl/kahm·byah·reh eel bahm·bee·noh*
Can you warm this?	**Me lo può scaldare?** *meh loh pwoh skahl·dah·reh*

For Traveling with Children, see page 143.

How to Complain

When will our food be ready?	**C'è ancora molto da aspettare?** *cheh ahn·koh·rah mohl·toh dah ah·speht·tah·reh*
We can't wait any longer.	**Non possiamo più aspettare.** *nohn pohs·syah·moh pyoo ah·speht·tah·reh*
We're leaving.	**Ce ne andiamo.** *cheh neh ahn·dyah·moh*
✓ I didn't order this.	**Non è quello che ho ordinato.** *nohn eh kwehl·loh keh oh ohr·dee·nah·toh*

I ordered...	**Ho ordinato...** oh ohr·dee·_nah_·toh...
I can't eat this.	**Non lo posso mangiare.** nohn loh _pohs_·soh mahn·_jyah_·reh
This is too...	**È troppo...** eh _trohp_·poh...
cold/hot	**freddo/caldo** _frehd_·doh/_kahl_·doh
salty/spicy	**salato/piccante** sah·_lah_·toh/peek·_kahn_·teh
tough/bland	**duro/insipido** _doo_·roh/een·_see_·pee·doh
This isn't clean/fresh.	**Non è pulito/fresco.** nohn eh poo·_lee_·toh/_freh_·skoh

Paying

The check [bill], please.	**Il conto, per favore.** eel _kohn_·toh pehr fah·_voh_·reh
Separate checks [bills], please.	**Conti separati, per favore.** _kohn_·tee seh·pah·_rah_·tee pehr fah·_voh_·reh
It's all together.	**Conto unico.** _kohn_·toh _oo_·nee·koh
Is service included?	**Il servizio è compreso?** eel sehr·_vee_·tsyoh eh kohm·_preh_·zoh
What's this amount for?	**Per cos'è questo importo?** pehr koh·_zeh_ _kweh_·stoh eem·_pohr_·toh
I didn't have that. I had...	**Questo non è mio. Io ho mangiato...** _kweh_·stoh nohn eh _mee_·oh _ee_·oh oh mahn·_jyah_·toh...
Can I have a receipt/ an itemized bill?	**Posso avere la fattura/il conto dettagliato?** _pohs_·soh ah·_veh_·reh lah faht·_too_·rah/ eel _kohn_·toh deht·tah·_llyah_·toh
That was delicious!	**Era squisito!** _eh_·rah skwee·_zee_·toh
I've already paid	**L'ho gia pagato** loh jyah pah·_gah_·toh

Restaurants charge a **coperto** (service charge) but tipping 10–15% of the bill is common for good service. Tipping is customary in finer restaurants.

Meals & Cooking

Breakfast

l'acqua *lah·kwah*	water
gli affettati *llyee ahf·feht·tah·tee*	cold cuts [charcuterie]
il burro *eel boor·roh*	butter
il caffè/tè... *eel kahf·feh/teh...*	coffee/tea...
con il dolcificante *kohn eel dohl·chee·fee·kahn·teh*	with artificial sweetener
al latte *ahl laht·teh*	with milk
con lo zucchero *kohn loh dzook·keh·roh*	with sugar
decaffeinato *deh·kahf·feh·ee·nah·toh*	decaf
nero *neh·roh*	black
i cereali *ee cheh·reh·ah·lee*	cereal
la farina d'avena *lah fah·ree·nah dah·veh·nah*	oatmeal
il formaggio *eel fohr·mah·djoh*	cheese
la frittata *lah freet·tah·tah*	omelet
il latte *eel laht·teh*	milk
la marmellata *lah mahr·mehl·lah·tah*	jam
il muesli *eel mweh·slee*	granola [muesli]
il muffin *eel mahf·feen*	muffin
la pancetta *lah pahn·cheht·tah*	bacon
il pane *eel pah·neh*	bread
il pane tostato *eel pah·neh toh·stah·toh*	toast
il panino *eel pah·nee·noh*	roll
la salsiccia *lah sahl·see·chyah*	sausage
il succo... *eel sook·koh...*	...juice
d'arancia *dah·rahn·chyah*	orange
di mela *dee meh·lah*	apple
di pompelmo *dee pohm·pehl·moh*	grapefruit

l'uovo... *lwoh•voh...* | ...egg
fritto *freet•toh* | fried
sodo/alla coque *soh•doh/ahl•lah kohk* | hard-/soft-boiled
strapazzato *strah•pah•tsah•toh* | scrambled
lo yogurt *loh yoh•goort* | yogurt

Appetizers

l'acciuga *lah•chyoo•ghah* | anchovy
l'affettato *lahf•feht•tah•toh* | platter of cold cuts
le alici a scapece *leh ah•lee•chee ah skah•peh•cheh* | fresh fried anchovies marinated in vinegar and spices
l'antipasto misto *lahn•tee•pah•stoh mee•stoh* | assorted appetizers
la bresaola *lah breh•sah•oh•lah* | cured raw beef
i carciofini sott'olio *ee kar•chyoh•fee•nee soht•toh•lyoh* | artichoke hearts in olive oil
la coppa *lah kohp•pah* | cured pork shoulder
i crostini *ee kroh•stee•nee* | toast topped with a variety of ingredients, including tomatoes, sardines and cheese
la caprese *lah kah•preh•seh* | sliced tomatoes, mozzarella and basil dressed with olive oil
l'insalata di frutti di mare *leen•sah•lah•tah dee froot•tee dee mah•reh* | seafood salad
la mortadella *lah mohr•tah•dehl•lah* | Bologna sausage
la peperonata *lah peh•peh•roh•nah•tah* | mixed sweet peppers stewed with tomatoes
il prosciutto crudo di Parma *eel proh•shyoot•toh kroo•doh dee pahr•mah* | cured ham from Parma
i sottaceti *ee soht•tah•cheh•tee* | pickled vegetables

Soup

l'acquacotta *lah·kwah·koht·tah* Tuscan vegetable soup with poached egg

il brodo di manzo *eel broh·doh dee mahn·dzoh* beef broth

il brodo di pollo *eel broh·doh dee pohl·loh* chicken broth

la buridda *lah boo·reed·dah* fish stew

il cacciucco *eel kah·chyook·koh* spicy seafood chowder

il cacciucco alla livornese *eel kah·chyook·koh ahl·lah lee·vohr·neh·seh* tomato seafood chowder

la crema di legumi *lah kreh·mah dee leh·goo·mee* vegetable cream soup

il minestrone *eel mee·neh·stroh·neh* mixed vegetable and bean soup

la ribollita *lah ree·bohl·lee·tah* Tuscan bean, vegetable and bread soup

lo spezzatino *loh speh·tsah·tee·noh* meat stew

la zuppa di fagioli *lah dzoop·pah dee fah·jyoh·lee* bean soup

la zuppa alla pavese *lah dzoop·pah ahl·lah pah·veh·seh* consommé with poached egg, croutons and grated cheese

la zuppa di pollo *lah dzoop·pah dee pohl·loh* chicken soup

la zuppa di pomodoro *lah dzoop·pah dee poh·moh·doh·roh* tomato soup

la zuppa di verdure *lah dzoop·pah dee vehr·doo·reh* vegetable soup

la zuppa di vongole *lah dzoop·pah dee vohn·goh·leh* clam and white wine soup

Fish & Seafood

l'acciuga *lah·chyoo·ghah* — anchovy

l'anguilla *lahn·gweel·lah* — eel

l'anguilla alla veneziana *lahn·gweel·lah ahl·lah veh·neh·tsyah·nah* — eel cooked in tomato sauce, a specialty of Venice

l'aragosta *lah·rah·goh·stah* — lobster

l'aringa *lah·reen·gah* — herring

il baccalà *eel bahk·kah·lah* — salted, dried cod

il branzino *eel brahn·dzee·noh* — sea bass

i calamari *ee kah·lah·mah·ree* — squid

le cozze *leh koh·tseh* — mussels

le cozze ripiene *leh koh·tseh ree·pyeh·neh* — stuffed mussels

il fritto misto *eel freet·toh mee·stoh* — mixed fried fish with shellfish

i gamberi *ee gahm·beh·ree* — shrimp

i gamberi grigliati *ee gahm·beh·ree gree·llyah·tee* — grilled shrimp with garlic

il granchio *eel grahn·kyoh* — crab

le lumache *leh loo·mah·keh* — snails

le lumache alla milanese *leh loo·mah·keh ahl·lah mee·lah·neh·seh* — snails with anchovy, fennel and wine sauce

il merluzzo *eel mehr·loo·tsoh* — cod

la moleca *lah moh·leh·kah* — soft shell crab

l'orata *loh·rah·tah* — sea bream

le ostriche *leh oh·stree·keh* — oysters

il pesce spada *eel peh·sheh spah·dah* — swordfish

il polpo *eel pohl·poh* — octopus

il salmone *eel sahl·moh·neh* — salmon

la sardina *lah sahr·dee·nah* — sardine

lo scorfano *loh skohr·fah·noh* — hog fish

la sogliola *lah soh·llyoh·lah* — sole

lo stoccafisso *loh stohk·kah·fees·soh* — dried cod cooked with tomatoes, olives and artichoke

il tonno *eel tohn·noh* — tuna
la trota *lah troh·tah* — trout
le vongole *leh vohn·goh·leh* — clams

Meat & Poultry

l'abbacchio alla romana *lahb·bahk·kyoh ahl·lah roh·mah·nah* — roasted spring lamb, a specialty of Rome
l'agnello *lah·nyehl·loh* — lamb
l'anatra *lah·nah·trah* — duck
la bistecca *lah bee·stehk·kah* — steak
la bistecca alla fiorentina *lah bee·stehk·kah ahl·lah fyoh·rehn·tee·nah* — grilled T-bone steak, a specialty of Florence
la braciola *lah brah·chyoh·lah* — grilled pork chop
il capretto *eel kah·preht·toh* — goat
la cima alla genovese *lah chee·mah ahl·lah jeh·noh·veh·seh* — flank steak stuffed with eggs and vegetables, a specialty of Genoa
il cinghiale *eel cheen·ghyah·leh* — wild boar, usually braised or roasted
il coniglio *eel koh·nee·llyoh* — rabbit
la cotoletta alla milanese *lah koh·toh·leht·tah ahl·lah mee·lah·neh·seh* — breaded veal cutlet flavored with cheese
la cotoletta di vitello con fontina *lah koh·toh·leht·tah dee vee·tehl·loh kohn fohn·tee·nah* — veal cutlet stuffed with fontina cheese, breaded and sautéed
il fagiano *eel fah·jyah·noh* — pheasant
il fegato *eel feh·gah·toh* — liver
il fegato alla veneziana *eel feh·gah·toh ahl·lah veh·neh·tsyah·nah* — thin slices of calf's liver fried with onions

il filetto al pepe verde *eel fee·leht·toh ahl peh·peh vehr·deh* — filet steak in a creamy sauce with green peppercorns

gli involtini *llyee een·vohl·tee·nee* — thin slices of meat rolled and stuffed

la luganega *lah loo·gah·neh·gah* — type of pork sausage

il maiale *eel mah·yah·leh* — pork

il manzo *eel mahn·dzoh* — beef

il montone *eel mohn·toh·neh* — mutton

l'oca *loh·kah* — goose

l'osso buco *lohs·soh boo·koh* — braised veal shank

la pancetta *lah pahn·cheht·tah* — bacon

la piccata al Marsala *lah peek·kah·tah ahl mahr·sah·lah* — thin cutlets cooked in Marsala sauce

il pollo *eel pohl·loh* — chicken

il pollo alla cacciatora *eel pohl·loh ahl·lah kah·chyah·toh·rah* — chicken braised with mushrooms in tomato sauce

il pollo alla diavola *eel pohl·loh ahl·lah dyah·voh·lah* — chicken grilled with lemon and hot pepper

il pollo al mattone *eel pohl·loh ahl maht·toh·neh* — chicken cooked with herbs in a brick oven

il pollo alla romana *eel pohl·loh ahl·lah roh·mah·nah* — diced chicken with tomato sauce and sweet peppers

la polpetta *lah pohl·peht·tah* — meatball

la porchetta *lah pohr·keht·tah* — suckling pig

il prosciutto *eel proh·shyoot·toh* — ham

la quaglia *lah kwah·llyah* — quail

la salsiccia *lah sahl·see·chyah* — sausage

il saltimbocca *eel sahl·teem·bohk·kah* — veal and ham roll

il tacchino *eel tahk·kee·noh* — turkey

il vitello *eel vee·tehl·loh* — veal

Vegetables & Staples

l'aceto *lah·cheh·toh*	vinegar
l'aglio *lah·llyoh*	garlic
l'asparago *lah·spah·rah·goh*	asparagus
l'avocado *lah·voh·kah·doh*	avocado
la barbabietola *lah bahr·bah·byeh·toh·lah*	beet
la bietola *lah byeh·toh·lah*	swiss chard
i broccoli *ee brohk·koh·lee*	broccoli
il carciofo *eel kahr·chyoh·foh*	artichoke
i carciofi alla guidea *ee kahr·chyoh·fee ahl·lah gwee·deh·ah*	crispy deep-fried artichokes, originally a specialty of the Jewish quarter in Rome
i carciofi alla romana *ee kahr·chyoh·fee ahl·lah roh·mah·nah*	whole lightly stewed artichokes stuffed with garlic, salt, olive oil, wild mint and parsley
la carota *lah kah·roh·tah*	carrot
il cavolfiore *eel kah·vohl·fyoh·reh*	cauliflower
il cavolo *eel kah·voh·loh*	cabbage
i ceci *ee cheh·chee*	chickpeas
il cetriolo *eel cheh·tryoh·loh*	cucumber
la cipolla *lah chee·pohl·lah*	onion
i fagioli *ee fah·jyoh·lee*	beans
i fagioli alla toscana *ee fah·jyoh·lee ahl·lah toh·skah·nah*	Tuscan-style beans seasoned with salt, black pepper and olive oil
i fagioli in umido *ee fah·jyoh·lee een oo·mee·doh*	beans cooked in tomato sauce and spices
i fagiolini *ee fah·jyoh·lee·nee*	green beans
le fave *leh fah·veh*	broad beans

i funghi *ee <u>foon</u>·ghee*		mushrooms
i funghi porcini arrostiti *ee <u>foon</u>·ghee*		porcini mushrooms
pohr·<u>chee</u>·nee ahr·roh·<u>stee</u>·tee		roasted or grilled with garlic, parsley and chili peppers
la lattuga *lah laht·<u>too</u>·gah*		lettuce
il mais *eel <u>mah</u>·ees*		corn
la melanzana *lah meh·lahn·<u>tsah</u>·nah*		eggplant [aubergine]
l'oliva *loh·<u>lee</u>·vah*		olive
l'ortaggio *lohr·<u>tah</u>·djoh*		vegetable
la pasta *lah <u>pah</u>·stah*		pasta
la patata *lah pah·<u>tah</u>·tah*		potato
il pepe bianco/nero *eel <u>peh</u>·peh <u>byahn</u>·koh/<u>neh</u>·roh*		white/black pepper
il pepe rosso *eel <u>peh</u>·peh <u>rohs</u>·soh*		paprika
il peperone rosso/verde *eel peh·peh·<u>roh</u>·neh <u>rohs</u>·soh/<u>vehr</u>·deh*		red/green pepper
i piselli *ee pee·<u>tsehl</u>·lee*		peas
i piselli al prosciutto *ee pee·<u>tsehl</u>·lee ahl proh·<u>shyoot</u>·toh*		peas with ham
la polenta *lah poh·<u>lehn</u>·tah*		cornmeal
la polenta al nero di seppia *lah poh·<u>lehn</u>·tah ahl <u>neh</u>·roh dee <u>sehp</u>·pyah*		polenta with baby squid in its own ink
il pomodoro *eel poh·moh·<u>doh</u>·roh*		tomato
i porri con le patate *ee <u>pohr</u>·ree kohn leh pah·<u>tah</u>·teh*		leek and potato casserole
la pizza *lah <u>pee</u>·tsah*		pizza
il riso *eel <u>ree</u>·zoh*		rice
il risotto *eel ree·<u>zoh</u>·toh*		arborio rice cooked slowly in broth, with seafood, vegetables, etc.
il sedano *eel seh·<u>dah</u>·noh*		celery

gli spinaci *llyee spee·nah·chee*   spinach
lo zucchero *loh tsook·keh·roh*   sugar
la zucchina *lah tsook·kee·nah*   zucchini [courgette]

In Italy, pizza is generally served in a size suitable for one person, though it can be shared. Pizza is usually thin crusted, about the size of a dinner plate, and is eaten with a knife and fork. Some pizzerias, though, may ask if you want your pizza **sottile** (thin) or **alta** (literally, high; here it means thick). There are many varieties of pizza and most are topped with mozzarella cheese; listed in the menu reader are some of the most popular.

Fruit

l'ananas *lah·nah·nahs*	pineapple
l'anguria *lahn·goo·ryah*	watermelon (northern Italy)
l'albicocca *lahl·bee·kohk·kah*	apricot
l'arancia *lah·rahn·chah*	orange
la banana *lah bah·nah·nah*	banana
il cedro *eel cheh·droh*	lime
la ciliegia *lah chee·lyeh·jyah*	cherry
il cocomero *eel koh·koh·meh·roh*	watermelon (Rome & southern Italy)
la fragola *lah frah·goh·lah*	strawberry
la frutta *lah froot·tah*	fruit
il lampone *eel lahm·poh·neh*	raspberry
il limone *eel lee·moh·neh*	lemon
la mela *lah meh·lah*	apple
il melone *eel meh·loh·neh*	melon

il mirtillo *eel meer·teel·loh*	blueberry
la pera *lah peh·rah*	pear
la pesca *lah peh·skah*	peach
il pompelmo *eel pohm·pehl·moh*	grapefruit
la prugna *lah proo·nyah*	plum
l'uva *loo·vah*	grape

Cheese

il formaggio... *eel fohr·mah·djoh...*	...cheese
asiago *ah·syah·goh*	nutty-flavored
Bel Paese *behl pah·eh·seh*	smooth and delicate
bocconcini *bohk·kohn·chee·nee*	small balls of fresh mozzarella
caciocavallo *kah·chyoh·kah·vahl·loh*	firm, slightly sweet, made with cow's or sheep's milk
caciotta *kah·chyoht·tah*	firm, usually mild
caprino *kah·pree·noh*	made from goat's milk
crescenza *kreh·shehn·tsah*	rich and creamy
dolce *dohl·cheh*	mild
dolcelatte *dohl·cheh·laht·teh*	mild, creamy, blue-veined
duro *doo·roh*	hard
fontina *fohn·tee·nah*	full-fat and semi-hard

gorgonzola *gohr·gohn·dzoh·lah* — strong and blue-veined
grana *grah·nah* — similar to parmesan
gruviera *groo·vyeh·rah* — sweet, nutlike flavor, similar to Swiss gruyere

mascarpone *mahs·kahr·poh·neh* — used like whipped cream
molle *mohl·leh* — soft
mozzarella *moh·tsah·rehl·lah* — full-fat and mild, made with cow's or buffalo's milk

parmigiano *pahr·mee·jyah·noh* — parmesan
pecorino *peh·koh·ree·noh* — strong, made with sheep's milk

piccante *peek·kahn·teh* — sharp
provolone *proh·voh·loh·neh* — firm and flavorful
ricotta *ree·koht·tah* — soft and mild, made with cow's or sheep's milk

Dessert

gli amaretti *llyee ah·mah·reht·tee* — almond cookies
il biscotto *eel bees·koht·toh* — crunchy cookie for dipping into coffee or wine
il budino *eel boo·dee·noh* — pudding
i cannoli *ee kahn·noh·lee* — crispy pastry tubes filled with sweetened ricotta and candied fruit
la cassata siciliana *lah kahs·sah·tah see·chee·lyah·nah* — traditional Sicilian cake with ricotta, chocolate and candied fruit
il castagnaccio *eel kah·stah·nyah·chyoh* — deep-fried chestnut cake
la crema *lah kreh·mah* — custard
la crostata *lah kroh·stah·tah* — pie
i dolci *ee dohl·chee* — sweets

il gelato *eel jeh·lah·toh* — ice cream

i gianduiotti *ee jyahn·dyoht·tee* — chocolate drops from Turin

la granita *lah grah·nee·tah* — frozen fruit-juice slush

il pandolce *eel pahn·dohl·cheh* — yeast cake with grapes and raisins

il panettone *eel pah·neht·toh·neh* — Christmas sweet bread with raisins and candied citrus peel

il panforte *eel pahn·fohr·teh* — dense cake made of almond, candied citrus, spices and honey

la panna cotta *lah pahn·nah koht·tah* — molded chilled cream pudding

il tartufo *eel tahr·too·foh* — chocolate truffle dessert

il tiramisù *eel tee·rah·mee·soo* — coffee- and rum-flavored layered dessert

la torta *lah tohr·tah* — cake

lo zabaglione *loh dzah·bah·llyoh·neh* — warm custard with Marsala wine

lo zuccotto *loh dzook·koht·toh* — sponge cake filled with fresh cream, chocolate, candied fruit and liqueur

The Italian **gelato**, similar to ice cream, is made from milk and sugar—not cream. Though it has less fat content than ice cream, it is still very dense and creamy. Popular flavors include **caffè** (coffee), **cioccolato** (chocolate), **fragola** (strawberry), **frutti di bosco** (mixed berries), **gianduia** (chocolate hazelnut), **limone** (lemon), **nocciola** (hazelnut), **pistacchio** (pistachio) and **vaniglia** (vanilla).

Sauces & Condiments

salt	**sale** *sah•leh*
pepper	**pepe** *peh•peh*
mustard	**senape** *seh•nah•peh*
ketchup	**ketchup** *keh•chyahp*

At the Market

Where are the carts [trolleys]/baskets?	**Dove sono i carrelli/cestini?** *doh•veh soh•noh ee kahr•rehl•lee/cheh•stee•nee*
Where is/ Where are…?	**Dov'è/Dove sono…?** *doh•veh/doh•veh soh•noh…*
I'd like some of that/this.	**Vorrei un po' di quello/questo.** *vohr•ray oon poh dee kwehl•loh/kweh•stoh*
Can I taste it?	**Posso assaggiarlo?** *pohs•soh ahs•sah•djahr•loh*
I'd like…	**Vorrei…** *vohr•ray…*
a kilo/half-kilo of…	**un chilo/mezzo chilo di…** *oon kee•loh/meh•dzoh kee•loh dee…*
a liter of…	**un litro di…** *oon lee•troh dee…*
a piece of…	**un pezzo di…** *oon peh•tsoh dee…*
a slice of…	**una fetta di…** *oo•nah feht•tah dee…*
More./Less.	**Di più./Di meno.** *dee pyoo/dee meh•noh*
How much?	**Quant'è?** *kwahn•teh*

Where do I pay?	**Dove si paga?** _doh_·veh see _pah_·gah
A bag, please.	**Una busta, per favore.** _oo_·nah _boos_·tah
	pehr fah·_voh_·reh
I'm being helped.	**Mi stanno servendo.** mee _stahn_·noh sehr·_vehn_·doh

Visit a **panetteria** (bakery) for fresh and tasty bread products; a **gastronomia** (delicatessen) for cold cuts, prepared meals sold by weight and fresh sandwiches; a **pasticceria** (pastry shop) for desserts; a **gelateria** (ice cream parlor) for ice cream specialties or a **bar** or **caffè** (cafe) for a variety of refreshments and small meals, which are cheaper if consumed standing, but more expensive for table service. You can find inexpensive food items at a local **supermercato** (supermarket).

YOU MAY HEAR...

Posso aiutarla? _pohs_·soh ah·yoo·_tahr_·lah	Can I help you?
Desidera? deh·_zee_·deh·rah	What would you like?
Altro? _ahl_·troh	Anything else?
Sono...euro. _soh_·noh...eh·oo·roh	That's...euros.

In the Kitchen

blender	**il frullatore** eel frool·lah·_toh_·reh
bottle opener	**l'apribottiglie** lah·pree·boht·_tee_·llyeh
bowl	**la coppa** lah _kohp_·pah
can opener	**l'apriscatole** lah·pree·_skah_·toh·leh

chopsticks	**i bastoncini cinesi** *ee bah·stohn·chee·nee chee·neh·see*
colander	**lo scolapasta** *lah skoh·lah·pah·stah*
corkscrew	**il cavatappi** *eel kah·vah·tahp·pee*
cup	**la tazza** *lah tah·tsah*
fork	**la forchetta** *lah fohr·keht·tah*
frying pan	**la padella** *lah pah·dehl·lah*
glass	**il bicchiere** *eel beek·kyeh·reh*
knife	**il coltello** *eel kohl·tehl·loh*
measuring cup/	**la tazza di misurazione/il misurino** *lah tah·tsah*
spoon	*dee mee·soo·rah·tsyoh·neh/eel mee·soo·ree·noh*
napkin	**il tovagliolo** *eel toh·vah·llyoh·loh*
plate	**il piatto** *eel pyaht·toh*
pot	**la pentola** *lah pehn·toh·lah*
spatula	**la spatola** *lah spah·toh·lah*
spoon	**il cucchiaio** *eel kook·kyah·yoh*

Measurements in Europe are metric - and that applies to the weight of food too. If you tend to think in pounds and ounces, it's worth brushing up on what the metric equivalent is before you go shopping for fruit and veg in markets and supermarkets. Five hundred grams, or half a kilo, is a common quantity to order, and that converts to just over a pound (17.65 ounces, to be precise).

YOU MAY SEE...

CALORIE	calories
SENZA GRASSI	fat free
CONSERVARE IN FRIGO	keep refrigerated
PUÒ CONTENERE TRACCE DI...	may contain traces of...
PUÒ ESSERE COTTO AL MICROONDE	microwaveable
DA CONSUMARE PREFERIBILMENTE ENTRO...	sell by...
ADATTO AI VEGETARIANI	suitable for vegetarians

Drinks

ESSENTIAL

Can I have the wine/ drink menu, please?
La carta dei vini/lista delle bevande, per favore. lah <u>kahr</u>•tah day <u>vee</u>•nee/<u>lee</u>•stah <u>dehl</u>•leh beh•<u>vahn</u>•deh pehr fah•<u>voh</u>•reh

What do you recommend?
Cosa mi consiglia? <u>koh</u>•zah mee kohn•<u>see</u>•llyah

I'd like a bottle/ glass of red/ white wine.
Vorrei una bottiglia/un bicchiere di vino rosso/bianco. vohr•<u>ray</u> oo•nah boht•<u>tee</u>•llyah/ oon beek•<u>kyeh</u>•reh dee <u>vee</u>•noh <u>rohs</u>•soh/<u>byahn</u>•koh

The house wine, please.
Il vino della casa, per favore. eel <u>vee</u>•noh <u>dehl</u>•lah <u>kah</u>•zah pehr fah•<u>voh</u>•reh

Another bottle/ glass, please.
Un'altra bottiglia/Un altro bicchiere, per favore. oo•<u>nahl</u>•trah boht•<u>tee</u>•llyah/oo•<u>nahl</u>•troh beek•<u>kyeh</u>•reh pehr fah•<u>voh</u>•reh

I'd like a local beer.
Vorrei una birra locale. vohr•<u>ray</u> oo•nah <u>beer</u>•rah loh•<u>kah</u>•leh

Cheers!
Salute! sah•<u>loo</u>•teh

Can I buy you a drink?	**Posso offrirle qualcosa?** _pohs•soh ohf•freer•leh kwahl•koh•sah_	
A coffee/tea, please.	**Un caffè/tè, per favore.** _oon kahf•feh/teh pehr fah•voh•reh_	
Black.	**Nero.** _neh•roh_	
With…	**Con…** _kohn…_	
some milk	**un po' di latte** _oon poh dee laht•teh_	
sugar	**lo zucchero** _loh dzook•keh•roh_	
artificial sweetener	**il dolcificante** _eel dohl•chee•fee•kahn•teh_	
…, please.	**…, per favore.** _…pehr fah•voh•reh_	
A juice	**Un succo** _oon sook•koh_	
A soda	**Una bibita** _oo•nah bee•bee•tah_	
A (sparkling/still) water	**Un bicchiere d'acqua (frizzante/naturale)** _oon beek•kyeh•reh dah•kwah (free•dzahn•teh/nah•too•rah•leh)_	

Non-alcoholic Drinks

l'acqua (frizzante/naturale) _lah•kwah (free•dzahn•teh/nah•too•rah•leh)_	water (sparkling/still)
la bibita _lah bee•bee•tah_	soda
il caffè _eel kahf•feh_	coffee
il latte _eel laht•teh_	milk
la limonata _lah lee•moh•nah•tah_	lemon soda
il succo _eel sook•koh_	juice
il tè (freddo) _eel teh (frehd•doh)_	(iced) tea
la spremuta _lah spreh•moo•tah_	fresh-squeezed fruit juice

Il caffè (coffee) has been a very popular drink in Italy since the 16th century, when the first European coffeehouse opened in Venice. Italians usually stop to drink a coffee—standing at the bar—on their way to work. If you have time to spare, you may wish to sit and enjoy your beverage, but you'll pay extra for table service. It is customary to have a cup of coffee after your meal. Popular types of Italian coffee include:

caffè: strong coffee, similar to espresso elsewhere
doppio: double serving of **caffè**
ristretto: very strong coffee, made with less water
americano: weak coffee, made with more water
macchiato: coffee served with steamed milk
cappuccino: equal parts coffee, steamed milk and milk foam

Aperitifs, Cocktails & Liqueurs

l'amaretto *lah·mah·reht·toh*	almond liqueur
l'amaro *lah·mah·roh*	bitter
il brandy *eel brahn·dee*	brandy
il digestivo *eel dee·jehs·tee·voh*	after-dinner drink

il gin *eel jeen*	gin
il rum *eel room*	rum
la sambuca *lah sahm·boo·kah*	aniseed-flavored liqueur
lo scotch *loh skohtch*	scotch
la strega *lah streh·gah*	sweet herb liqueur
la tequila *la teh·kee·lah*	tequila
la vodka *la vohd·kah*	vodka
il whisky *eel whees·kee*	whisky

YOU MAY HEAR...

Posso offrirle qualcosa?
pohs·soh ohf·freer·leh kwahl·koh·zah
Can I get you a drink?

Con latte o zucchero?
kohn laht·teh oh dzook·keh·roh
With milk or sugar?

Acqua frizzante o naturale? *ah·kwah*
free·dzahn·teh oh nah·too·rah·leh
Sparkling or still water?

Beer

la birra... *lah beer·rah...*	...beer
in bottiglia/alla spina *een boht·tee·llyah/ahl·lah spee·nah*	bottled/draft
scura/chiara *skoo·rah/kyah·rah*	dark/light
lager/pilsner *lah·gehr/peels·nehr*	lager/pilsner
nazionale/importata *nah·tsyoh·nah·leh/eem·pohr·tah·tah*	local/imported
analcolica *ah·nahl·koh·lee·kah*	non-alcoholic

Wine

lo champagne *loh shahm•pah•nyeh*	champagne
il vino… *eel vee•noh…*	…wine
rosso/bianco *rohs•soh/byahn•koh*	red/white
della casa/da tavola *dehl•lah kah•zah/dah tah•voh•lah*	house/table
secco/dolce *sehk•koh/dohl•cheh*	dry/sweet
frizzante *free•dzahn•teh*	sparkling
da dessert *dah dehs•sehrt*	dessert

Popular types of Italian wine are listed below. The region where the wine is typically found is listed in parentheses.

sparkling sweet wine	Asti spumante (Piedmont); Prosecco (Veneto)
red wine	Nebbiolo (Piedmont); Amarone, Valpolicella (Veneto); Brunello di Montalcino, Chianti, Sangiovese (Tuscany); Corvo Rosso, Nero d'Avola (Sicily)
rosé	Lagrein (Trentino-Alto Adige)
dry white wine	Frascati (Latium); Orvieto (Umbria); Pinot grigio (Veneto); Vermentino (Sardinia)
dessert wine	Vin santo (Tuscany)

l'abbacchio *lahb-bahk-kyoh* — lamb

l'acciuga *lah-chyoo-ghah* — anchovy

l'aceto *lah-cheh-toh* — vinegar

l'aceto balsamico *lah-cheh-toh bahl-sah-mee-koh* — balsamic vinegar

l'acqua *lah-kwah* — water

l'acqua tonica *lah-kwah toh-nee-kah* — tonic water

gli affettati *llyee ahf-feht-tah-tee* — cold cuts [charcuterie]

l'agliata *lah-llyah-tah* — garlic sauce

l'aglio *lah-llyoh* — garlic

l'agnello *lah-nyehl-loh* — lamb

l'albicocca *lahl-bee-kohk-kah* — apricot

l'albume *lahl-boo-meh* — egg white

gli alcolici *llyee ahl-koh-lee-chee* — spirits

l'alloro *lahl-loh-roh* — bay leaf

l'amarena *lah-mah-reh-nah* — sour cherry

l'ananas *lah-nah-nahs* — pineapple

l'anatra *lah-nah-trah* — duck

l'aneto *lah-neh-toh* — dill

l'anguilla *lahn-gweel-lah* — eel

l'anguria *lahn-goo-ryah* — watermelon (northern Italy)

l'aperitivo *lah-peh-ree-tee-voh* — aperitif

l'arachide *lah-rah-kee-deh* — peanut

l'aragosta *lah-rah-goh-stah* — lobster

l'arancia *lah-rahn-chyah* — orange

l'aringa *lah-reen-gah* — herring

l'arrosto *lahr-roh-stoh* — roast

gli aromi *llyee ah-roh-mee* — herbs

l'asparago *lah-spah-rah-goh* — asparagus

l'avocado *lah·voh·kah·doh* — avocado

il baccalà *eel bahk·kah·lah* — salted, dried cod

la banana *lah bah·nah·nah* — banana

la barbabietola *lah bahr·bah·byeh·toh·lah* — beet

il basilico *eel bah·see·lee·koh* — basil

la bibita *lah bee·bee·tah* — soda

la bietola *lah byeh·toh·lah* — swiss chard

la birra *lah beer·rah* — beer

il biscotto *eel bee·skoht·toh* — cookie [biscuit]

la bistecca *lah bee·stehk·kah* — steak

la braciola *lah brah·chyoh·lah* — grilled pork chop

il brandy *eel brahn·dee* — brandy

il branzino *eel brahn·dzee·noh* — sea bass

i broccoli *ee brohk·koh·lee* — broccoli

il brodo *eel broh·doh* — broth

il budino *eel boo·dee·noh* — pudding

il bue *eel boo·eh* — ox

la burrida *lah boo·reed·dah* — fish stew (Genova)

il burro *eel boor·roh* — butter

il caffè *eel kahf·feh* — coffee

i calamari *ee kah·lah·mah·ree* — squid

la cannella *lah kahn·nehl·lah* — cinnamon

il cappero *eel kahp·peh·roh* — caper

la capra *lah kah·prah* — goat

il capretto *eel kah·preht·toh* — kid (baby goat)

le caramelle *leh kah·rah·mehl·leh* — candy [sweets]

il caramello *eel kah·rah·mehl·loh* — caramel

il carciofo *eel kahr·chyoh·foh* — artichoke

i cardi *ee kahr·dee* — cardoons (relative of the artichoke)

la carne *lah kahr·neh* — meat

la carne in scatola *lah kahr·neh een skah·toh·lah* — corned beef

la carne tritata *lah kahr·neh tree·tah·tah* — ground meat

la carota *lah kah·roh·tah* — carrot

la castagna *lah kah·stah·nyah* — chestnut

il cavolfiore *eel kah·vohl·fyoh·reh* — cauliflower

i cavoletti di Bruxelles *ee kah·voh·leht·tee dee broo·ksehl* — Brussels sprouts

il cavolo *eel kah·voh·loh* — cabbage

il cavolo rosso *eel kah·voh·loh rohs·soh* — red cabbage

i ceci *ee cheh·chee* — chickpeas

il cedro *eel cheh·droh* — lime

i cereali *ee cheh·reh·ah·lee* — cereal

il cervo *eel chehr·voh* — venison

il cetriolino *eel cheh·tryoh·lee·noh* — gherkin

il cetriolo *eel cheh·tryoh·loh* — cucumber

la ciambella fritta *lah chahm·behl·lah freet·tah* — doughnut

il chiodo di garofano *eel kyoh·doh dee gah·roh·fah·noh* — clove

la cicoria *lah chee·koh·ryah* — chicory

la ciliegia *lah chee·lyeh·jyah* — cherry

il cinghiale *eel cheen·ghyah·leh* — wild boar

il cioccolato *eel chyohk·koh·lah·toh* — chocolate

la cipolla *lah chee·pohl·lah* — onion

la cipollina verde *lah chee·pohl·lee·nah vehr·deh* — scallion [spring onion]

il cocco *eel kohk·koh* — coconut

il cocomero *eel koh·koh·meh·roh* — watermelon (Rome and southern Italy)

la coda di bue *lah koh·dah dee boo·eh* — oxtail

la confettura *lah kohn·feht·too·rah*	jam
il coniglio *eel koh·nee·llyoh*	rabbit
la conserva *lah kohn·sehr·vah*	tomato paste
il consommé *eel kohn·sohm·meh*	consommé
la coppa *lah kohp·pah*	cured pork shoulder
il cornetto *eel kohr·neht·toh*	croissant
la coscia *lah koh·shah*	leg
le cozze *leh koh·tseh*	mussel
il cracker *eel krah·kehr*	cracker
i crauti *ee krawoo·tee*	sauerkraut
la crema *lah kreh·mah*	custard
il crescione *eel kreh·shyoh·neh*	watercress
le crespelle *leh kreh·spehl·leh*	crepes
la crostata *lah kroh·stah·tah*	pie
il cumino *eel koo·mee·noh*	caraway/cumin
i datteri *ee daht·teh·ree*	dates
il digestivo *eel dee·jeh·stee·voh*	after-dinner drink
il dolcificante *eel dohl·chee·fee·kahn·teh*	sweetener
il dragoncello *eel drah·gohn·chehl·loh*	tarragon
l'erba cipollina *lehr·bah chee·pohl·lee·nah*	chives
l'erbetta *lehr·beht·teh*	herb

l'espresso *leh·sprehs·soh* — coffee

il fagiano *eel fah·jyah·noh* — pheasant

il fagiolino *eel fah·jyoh·lee·noh* — green bean

i fagioli di soya *ee fah·jyoh·dee soh·yah* — soybean [soya bean]

il fagiolo *eel fah·jyoh·loh* — bean

la faraona *lah fah·rah·oh·nah* — guinea fowl

la farina *lah fah·ree·nah* — flour

la farina d'avena *lah fah·ree·nah dah·veh·nah* — oatmeal

la farina di mais *lah fah·ree·nah dee mah·ees* — cornmeal

il fegato *eel feh·gah·toh* — liver

il filetto *eel fee·leht·toh* — filet

il fico *eel fee·koh* — fig

il finocchio *eel fee·nohk·kyoh* — fennel

il formaggio *eel fohr·mah·djoh* — cheese

il formaggio caprino *eel fohr·mah·djoh kah·pree·noh* — goat cheese

il formaggio cremoso *eel fohr·mah·djoh kreh·moh·zoh* — cream cheese

i fiocchi di latte *ee fyohk·kee dee laht·teh* — cottage cheese

la fragola *lah frah·goh·lah* — strawberry

la frittata *lah freet·tah·tah* — omelet

la frittella *lah freet·tehl·lah* — fritter/pancake

il frullatto *eel frool·lah·toh* — milkshake

la frutta *lah froot·tah* — fruit

la frutta cotta *lah froot·tah koht·tah* — stewed fruit

i frutti di bosco *ee froot·tee dee boh·skoh* — mixed berries

i frutti di mare *ee froot·tee dee mah·reh* — seafood/shellfish

il fungo *eel foon·goh* — mushroom

la gallina *lah gahl·lee·nah* — hen

il gambero *eel gahm·beh·roh* — shrimp

la gelatina *lah jeh·lah·tee·nah* — jelly

il gelato *eel jeh-lah-toh* — ice cream

il germoglio di soia *eel jehr-moh-llyoh dee soh-yah* — bean sprouts

il ghiaccio *eel ghyah-chyoh* — ice (cube)

il gin *eel geen* — gin

il gorgonzola *eel gohr-gohn-dzoh-lah* — blue cheese

il granchio *eel grahn-kyoh* — crab

il grano *eel grah-noh* — wheat

la guava *lah gwah-vah* — guava

l'hamburger *lahm-boor-gehr* — hamburger

l'indivia *leen-dee-vyah* — endive

l'insalata *leen-sah-lah-tah* — salad

il ketchup *eel keht-choop* — ketchup

il kiwi *eel kee-wee* — kiwi

il lampone *eel lahm-poh-neh* — raspberry

il latte *eel laht-teh* — milk

il latte di soia *eel laht-teh dee soh-yah* — soymilk [soya milk]

la lattuga *lah laht-too-gah* — lettuce

la lenticchia *lah lehn-teek-kyah* — lentil

la limonata *lah lee-moh-nah-tah* — lemon soda

il limone *eel lee-moh-neh* — lemon

la lingua *lah leen-gwah* — tongue

il liquore *eel lee-kwoh-reh* — liqueur

il liquore all'arancia *eel lee-kwoh-reh ahl-lah-rahn-chyah* — orange liqueur

il lombo *eel lohm-boh* — loin/sirloin

la lumaca *lah loo-mah-kah* — snail

i maccheroni *ee mahk-keh-roh-nee* — macaroni

il maiale *eel mah-yah-leh* — pork

il maialino da latte *eel mah-yah-lee-noh dah laht-teh* — suckling pig

la maionese *lah mah·yoh·neh·zeh*	mayonnaise
il mais dolce *eel mah·ees dohl·cheh*	sweet corn
il mandarino *eel mahn·dah·ree·noh*	tangerine
la mandorla *lah mahn·dohr·lah*	almond
il mango *eel mahn·goh*	mango
il manzo *eel mahn·dzoh*	beef
la margarina *lah mahr·gah·ree·nah*	margarine
la marmellata *lah mahr·mehl·lah·tah*	marmalade/jam
il marzapane *eel mahr·dzah·pah·neh*	marzipan
la mela *lah meh·lah*	apple
la melanzana *lah meh·lahn·tsah·nah*	eggplant [aubergine]
il melograno *eel meh·loh·grah·noh*	pomegranate
il melone *eel meh·loh·neh*	melon
la menta *lah mehn·tah*	mint
la merenda *lah meh·rehn·dah*	snack
la meringa *lah meh·reen·gah*	meringue
il merluzzo *eel mehr·loo·tsoh*	cod
il miele *eel myeh·leh*	honey
il minestrone *eel mee·neh·stroh·neh*	vegetable and bean soup
il mirtillo *eel meer·teel·loh*	blueberry
il montone *eel mohn·toh·neh*	mutton
la mora *lah moh·rah*	blackberry
la mortadella *lah mohr·tah·dehl·lah*	Bologna sausage
il muesli *eel mweh·slee*	granola [muesli]
il muffin *eel mahf·feen*	muffin
il nasello *eel nah·zehl·loh*	hake
la nocciola *lah noh·chyoh·lah*	hazelnut
la noce *lah noh·cheh*	walnut
la noce moscata *lah noh·cheh moh·skah·tah*	nutmeg

la nutella *lah noo·tehl·lah* — hazelnut-flavored chocolate spread

l'oca *loh·kah* — goose

l'olio d'oliva *loh·lyoh doh·lee·vah* — olive oil

l'oliva *loh·lee·vah* — olive

l'orata *loh·rah·tah* — sea bream

l'origano *loh·ree·gah·noh* — oregano

l'ortaggio *lohr·tah·djoh* — vegetable

l'orzo *lohr·tsoh* — barley

l'ostrica *loh·stree·kah* — oyster

il palombo *eel pah·lohm·boh* — dogfish

la pancetta *lah pahn·cheht·tah* — bacon

il pane *eel pah·neh* — bread

il pane tostato *eel pah·neh toh·stah·toh* — toast

il panino *eel pah·nee·noh* — roll/sandwich

la panna acida *lah pahn·nah ah·chee·dah* — sour cream

la panna montata *lah pahn·nah mohn·tah·tah* — whipped cream

la papaya *lah pah·pah·yah* — papaya

la pasta *lah pah·stah* — pastry

pasta *pah·stah* — pasta

  gli agnolotti *llyee ah·nyoh·loht·tee* — meat-stuffed pasta

  i cannelloni *ee kahn·nehl·loh·nee* — stuffed pasta tubes, topped with sauce

  i cappelletti *ee kahp·pehl·leht·tee* — small ravioli filled with meat, ham, cheese and eggs

  i capelli d'angelo *ee kah·pehl·lee dahn·jeh·loh* — angelhair pasta

  le fettuccine *leh feht·too·chee·neh* — broad, long pasta made from eggs and flour

  i fusilli *ee foo·seel·lee* — spiral-shaped pasta

gli gnocchi *llyee nyohk·kee* — small potato dumplings
le lasagne *leh lah·sah·nyeh* — thin pasta strips layered with tomato or white sauce, meat and cheese

le linguine *leh leen·gwee·neh* — narrow, long pasta
le orecchiette *leh oh·reh·kyeht·teh* — small, shell-shaped pasta
i pansotti *ee pahn·soht·tee* — swiss chard- and herb-stuffed pasta, usually served with a walnut sauce

le pappardelle *leh pahp·pahr·dehl·leh* — long, rectangula pasta of medium width with ribbon edges

la pastina *lah pahs·tee·nah* — tiny, dried pasta used in soups
le penne *leh pehn·neh* — short, tubular pasta with angled ends

i quadrucci *ee kwah·droo·chee* — stuffed pasta squares added to soup

i rigatoni *ee ree·gah·toh·nee* — fat tubes of dried pasta with ridges

gli spaghetti *llyee spah·gheht·tee* — long thin strands of fresh pasta

le tagliatelle *leh tah·llyah·tehl·leh* — thin, long pasta with ribbon edges

i tortelli *ee tohr·tehl·lee* — stuffed rectangular or square fresh pasta

i tortellini *ee tohr·tehl·lee·nee* — small stuffed pasta nuggets
gli ziti *llyee tsee·tee* — tubular pasta
il pasticcio *pah·stee·chyoh* — pie
la pastina *lah pah·stee·nah* — tiny dried pasta used in soups

pasta... _pah_·stah	pasta with...
all'agliata ahl·lah·_llyah_·tah	hot and spicy sauce with garlic
all'Alfredo ahl·lahl·_freh_·doh	butter and parmesan cheese
all'amatriciana ahl·lah·mah·tree·_chyah_·nah	bacon and tomato
alla bolognese _ahl_·lah boh·loh·_nyeh_·seh	ground meat and tomato
alla boscaiola _ahl_·lah boh·skah·_yoh_·lah	tomatoes, butter, cheese, mushrooms, olive oil and garlic
alla carbonara _ahl_·lah kahr·boh·_nah_·rah	bacon and egg
fra' diavolo frah _dyah_·voh·loh	tomato with hot pepper
alla marinara _ahl_·lah mah·ree·_nah_·rah	tomato, olive oil and garlic
alla napoletana _ahl_·lah nah·poh·leh·_tah_·nah	cheese, tomatoes and herbs
al pesto ahl _peh_·stoh	ground basil, garlic, parmesan and pine nuts
al pomodoro ahl poh·moh·_doh_·roh	simple tomato sauce
alla puttanesca _ahl_·lah poot·tah·_neh_·skah	tomatoes, black olives, peppers, olive oil and garlic
al ragù ahl rah·_goo_	with meat

alla siciliana _ahl·lah see·chee·lyah·nah_	provolone and eggplant
alle vongole _ahl·leh vohn·goh·leh_	clams and tomato
la patata _lah pah·tah·tah_	potato
la patata americana _lah pah·tah·tah ah·meh·ree·kah·nah_	sweet potato
le patatine _leh pah·tah·tee·neh_	potato chips [crisps]
le patatine fritte _leh pah·tah·tee·neh freet·teh_	French fries
il paté _eel pah·teh_	pâté
il pepe _eel peh·peh_	pepper (seasoning)
il pepe bianco _eel peh·peh byahn·koh_	white pepper (seasoning)
il pepe nero _eel peh·peh neh·roh_	black pepper (seasoning)
il pepe rosso _eel peh·peh rohs·soh_	paprika
il peperoncino _eel peh·peh·rohn·chee·noh_	chili pepper
il peperone _eel peh·peh·roh·neh_	pepper (vegetable)
la pera _lah peh·rah_	pear
il persico _eel pehr·see·koh_	fresh water perch
la pesca _lah peh·skah_	peach
il pesce _eel peh·sheh_	fish
il pesce spada _eel peh·sheh spah·dah_	swordfish
il pettine di mare _eel peht·tee·neh dee mah·reh_	scallop
il petto (di pollo) _eel peht·toh (dee pohl·loh)_	breast (of chicken)
i pinoli _ee pee·noh·lee_	pine nuts
il piselli _eel pee·zehl·lee_	peas
il pesto _eel peh·stoh_	sauce made with basil, garlic, parmesan and pinenuts
la pizza... _lah pee·tsah..._	...pizza
bianca _byahn·kah_	'white,' without tomato sauce
con i funghi _kohn ee foon·ghee_	with mushrooms
dolce _dohl·cheh_	with a variety of sweet toppings, served as a dessert

margherita *mahr·gheh·ree·tah* — tomato, cheese and basil or oregano, named after Italy's first queen and reflecting the national colors

marinara *mah·ree·nah·rah* — with tomato sauce, garlic, capers, oregano and sometimes anchovies

napoletana *nah·poh·leh·tah·nah* — anchovies, tomatoes, cheese and sometimes capers

quattro formaggi *kwaht·troh fohr·mah·djee* — with four types of cheese

quattro stagioni *kwaht·troh stah·jyoh·nee* — 'four seasons', with tomatoes, artichokes, mushrooms, olives; plus cheese, ham and bacon

rustica *roos·tee·kah* — with ricotta, mozzarella, prosciutto, mortadella and seasonings

il pollame *eel pohl·lah·meh* — poultry

il pollo *eel pohl·loh* — chicken

la polenta *lah poh·lehn·tah* — cornmeal

la polpa di granchio *lah pohl·pah dee grahn·kyoh* — crabmeat

la polpetta *lah pohl·peht·tah* — meatball

il polpo *eel pohl·poh* — octopus

il pomodoro *eel poh·moh·doh·roh* — tomato

il pompelmo *eel pohm·pehl·moh* — grapefruit

i porcini *ee pohr·chee·nee* — porcini mushrooms

la porchetta *lah pohr·keht·tah* — suckling pig

il porro *eel pohr·roh* — leek

il porto *eel pohr·toh* — port

il prezzemolo *eel preh·tseh·moh·loh*	parsley
il prosciutto *eel proh·shyoot·toh*	ham
la prugna *lah proo·nyah*	plum
la prugna secca *lah proo·nyah sehk·kah*	prune
le puntarelle *leh poon·tah·rehl·leh*	wild chicory
la quaglia *lah kwah·llyah*	quail
il rabarbaro *eel rah·bahr·bah·roh*	rhubarb
il radicchio *eel rah·deek·kyoh*	red chicory
il ravanello *eel rah·vah·nehl·loh*	radish
la rana *lah rah·nah*	frog
la rana pescatrice *lah rah·nah peh·skah·tree·cheh*	monkfish
la rapa *lah rah·pah*	turnip
il ribes nero *eel ree·behs neh·roh*	black currant
il ribes rosso *eel ree·behs rohs·soh*	red currant
il riccio di mare *eel ree·chyoh dee mah·reh*	sea urchin
le rigaglie *leh ree·gah·llyeh*	giblet
il riso *eel ree·zoh*	rice
il risotto *eel ree·zoht·toh*	rice cooked in broth
il rosbif *eel rohz·beef*	roast beef
il rosmarino *eel rohz·mah·ree·noh*	rosemary
il rum *eel room*	rum
il salame *eel sah·lah·meh*	salami
il sale *eel sah·leh*	salt
il salmone *eel sahl·moh·neh*	salmon
la salsa *lah sahl·sah*	sauce
la salsa agrodolce *lah sahl·sah*	sweet and sour sauce
la salsa piccante *lah sahl·sah peek·kahn·teh*	hot pepper sauce
la salsa di soia *lah sahl·sah dee soh·yah*	soy sauce
la salsiccia *lah sahl·see·chyah*	sausage
la salvia *lah sahl·vyah*	sage

il sanguinaccio *eel sahn·gwee·nah·chyoh*	blood sausage
le sardine *leh sahr·dee·neh*	sardine
i savoiardi *ee sah·voh·yahr·dee*	'ladyfingers', small sponge cakes used to make tiramisu
lo scalogno *loh skah·loh·nyoh*	shallot
la scarola *lah skah·roh·lah*	escarole
lo sciroppo *loh shee·rohp·poh*	syrup
lo scotch *loh skohtch*	scotch
il sedano *eel seh·dah·noh*	celery
la segale *lah seh·gah·leh*	rye
la selvaggina *lah sehl·vah·djee·nah*	game
i semi di finocchio *ee seh·mee dee fee·nohk·kyoh*	fennel seeds
la senape *lah seh·nah·peh*	mustard
lo scombro *loh skohm·broh*	mackerel
lo sherry *loh shehr·ree*	sherry
la sogliola *lah soh·llyoh·lah*	sole
la soia *lah soh·yah*	soy [soya]
il sottaceto *eel soht·tah·cheh·toh*	pickle
la spalla *lah spahl·lah*	shoulder
le spezie *leh speh·tsyeh*	spices
lo spezzatino *loh speh·tsah·tee·noh*	meat stew
gli spinaci *llyee spee·nah·chee*	spinach
la spremuta *lah spreh·muh·tah*	fresh-squeezed juice
lo stinco *loh steen·koh*	shank
lo strutto *loh stroot·toh*	lard
il succo *eel sook·koh*	juice
il tacchino *eel tahk·kee·noh*	turkey
il tartufo *eel tahr·too·foh*	truffles
il tè *eel teh*	tea
il timo *eel tee·moh*	thyme

il tofu *eel <u>toh</u>·foo*	tofu
il tonno *eel <u>tohn</u>·noh*	tuna
il torrone *eel tohr·<u>roh</u>·neh*	nougat
la torta *lah <u>tohr</u>·tah*	cake
la triglia *lah <u>tree</u>·llyah*	red mullet
la trippa *lah <u>treep</u>·pah*	tripe
la trota *lah <u>troh</u>·tah*	trout
il tuorlo *eel <u>twohr</u>·loh*	egg yolk
l'uovo *<u>lwoh</u>·voh*	egg
l'uva *<u>loo</u>·vah*	grape
l'uva spina *<u>loo</u>·vah <u>spee</u>·nah*	gooseberry
l'uvetta *loo·<u>veht</u>·tah*	raisin
la vaniglia *lah vah·<u>nee</u>·llyah*	vanilla
il vermouth *eel <u>vehr</u>·mooth*	vermouth
la verdura *lah vehr·<u>doo</u>·rah*	vegetable
il vino *eel <u>vee</u>·noh*	wine
il vino da dessert *eel <u>vee</u>·noh dah dehs·<u>sehrt</u>*	dessert wine
il vitello *eel vee·<u>tehl</u>·loh*	veal
la vodka *lah <u>vohd</u>·kah*	vodka
la vongola *lah <u>vohn</u>·goh·lah*	clam
il wafer *eel <u>vah</u>·fehr*	waffle
il whisky *eel <u>whee</u>·skee*	whisky
il wurstel *eel <u>voor</u>·stehl*	hot dog
lo yogurt *loh <u>yoh</u>·goort*	yogurt
lo zafferano *loh dzahf·feh·<u>rah</u>·noh*	saffron
lo zenzero *loh <u>dzehn</u>·dzeh·roh*	ginger
la zucca *lah <u>dzook</u>·kah*	squash
lo zucchero *loh <u>dzook</u>·keh·roh*	sugar
la zucchina *lah <u>dzook</u>·kee·nah*	zucchini [courgette]
la zuppa *lah <u>dzoop</u>·pah*	soup

People

ESSENTIAL

Hello!/Hi!	**Salve!/Ciao!** _sahl_•veh/_chah_•oh
How are you?	**Come sta?** _koh_•meh stah
Fine, thanks.	**Bene, grazie.** _beh_•neh _grah_•tsyeh
Excuse me!	**Scusi!** _skoo_•zee
Do you speak English?	**Parla inglese?** _pahr_•lah een•_gleh_•zeh
What's your name?	**Come si chiama?** _koh_•meh see _kyah_•mah
My name is...	**Mi chiamo...** mee _kyah_•moh...
Nice to meet you.	**Piacere.** pyah•_cheh_•reh ✓
Where are you	**Di dov'è?** dee doh•_veh_ from? ✓
I'm American.	**Sono Americano _m_/Americana** ✓
	soh•noh ah•meh•ree•_kah_•noh/ah•meh•ree•_kah_•nah
I'm British.	**Sono inglese.** _soh_•noh een•_gleh_•zeh
What do you do for	**Cosa fa?** _koh_•zah fah
a living?	
I work for...	**Lavoro per...** lah•_voh_•roh pehr...
I'm a student.	**Studio.** _stoo_•dyoh
I'm retired.	**Sono in pensione.** _soh_•noh een pehn•_syoh_•neh ✓
Do you like...?	**Le piace...?** leh _pyah_•cheh... ✓
Goodbye.	**Arrivederla.** ahr•ree•veh•_dehr_•lah
See you later.	**A dopo.** ah _doh_•poh

Language Difficulties

Do you speak English?	**Parla inglese?** _pahr_•lah een•_gleh_•zeh
Does anyone here speak English?	**Qualcuno parla inglese?** kwahl•_koo_•noh _pahr_•lah een•_gleh_•zeh

Italians have many greetings. The following are the most commonly used forms and when to use them.

buongiorno: literally, good day; this greeting is used from morning to mid-afternoon

salve: a formal hello ✓

ciao: an informal hi or bye

buon pomeriggio: good afternoon

buonasera: good evening; used from late afternoon until late in the evening

buonanotte: good night; used late in the evening or at bedtime

arrivederla: formal goodbye

arrivederci: informal goodbye

I don't speak (much) Italian.	**Non parlo (molto bene l') italiano.** *nohn pahr·loh (mohl·toh beh·neh l) ee·tah·lyah·noh*
Can you speak more slowly?	**Può parlare più lentamente?** *pwoh pahr·lah·reh pyoo lehn·tah·mehn·teh*
Can you repeat that?	**Può ripetere?** *pwoh ree·peh·teh·reh*
Excuse me?	**Come?** *koh·meh*
What was that?	**Cosa ha detto?** *koh·zah ah deht·toh*
Can you spell it?	**Come si scrive?** *koh·meh see skree·veh*
Can you write it down?	**Me lo può scrivere?** *meh loh pwo skree·veh·reh*
Can you translate this into English for me?	**Può tradurlo in inglese?** *pwoh trah·door·loh een een·gleh·zeh*
What does... mean?	**Che significa...?** *keh see·nyee·fee·kah...*
I understand.	**Capisco.** *kah·pee·skoh*
I don't understand.	**Non capisco.** *nohn kah·pee·skoh*
Do you understand?	**Capisce?** *kah·pee·sheh*

Making Friends

Hello!	**Salve!** _sahl_·veh
Good morning.	**Buongiorno.** bwohn·_jyohr_·noh
Good afternoon.	**Buon pomeriggio.** bwohn poh·meh·_ree_·djoh
Good evening.	**Buonasera.** bwoh·nah·_seh_·rah
My name is…	**Mi chiamo…** mee _kyah_·moh…
What's your name?	**Come si chiama?** _koh_·meh see _kyah_·mah
I'd like to introduce you to…	**Le presento…** leh preh·_zehn_·toh…
Pleased to meet you.	**Piacere.** pyah·_cheh_·reh
How are you?	**Come sta?** _koh_·meh stah
Fine, thanks. And you?	**Bene, grazie. E Lei?** _beh_·neh _grah_·tsyeh eh lay

Signore (Mr.), **Signora** (Mrs.), **Signorina** (Miss) and professional titles - **Dottore** (Dr.), **Professore** (Professor) - are frequently used, even when you don't know the person's last name. When trying to get someone's attention, you don't have to include his or her title; a simple **Scusi!** (formal) or **Scusa!** (informal) is sufficient.

YOU MAY HEAR...

Parlo poco inglese. _pahr_•loh _poh_•koh
een•_gleh_•zeh

I only speak a little
English.

Non parlo inglese. nohn _pahr_•loh
een•_gleh_•zeh

I don't speak English.

Travel Talk

I'm here...	**Sono qui...** _soh_•noh kwee... ✓
on business	**per lavoro** pehr lah•_voh_•roh
on vacation	**in vacanza** een vah•_kahn_•tsah ✓
studying	**per studio** pehr _stoo_•dyoh
I'm staying for...	**Rimango...** ree•_mahn_•goh...
I've been here...	**Sono qui da...** _soh_•noh kwee dah...
a day	**un giorno** oon _jyohr_•noh
a week	**una settimana** _oo_•nah seht•tee•_mah_•nah
a month	**un mese** oon _meh_•zeh
Where are you from?	**Di dove sei?** dee doh•_veh_ seh•ee
I'm from...	**Sono di...** _soh_•noh dee...

For Numbers, see page 167.

Personal

Who are you with?	**Con chi è?** _kohn kee ee_
I'm here alone.	**Sono da solo** m **/sola** f _soh_•noh dah _soh_•loh/_soh_•lah
I'm with my...	**Sono con...** _soh_•noh kohn...
husband/wife	**mio marito** m **/mia moglie** f _mee_•oh mah•_ree_•toh/ _mee_•ah moh•llyeh
boyfriend/ girlfriend	**il mio ragazzo** m **/la mia ragazza** f eel _mee_•oh rah•_gah_•tsoh/lah _mee_•ah rah•_gah_•tsah
a friend	**un amico** m **/un'amica** f oon ah•_mee_•koh/ oo•nah•_mee_•kah
friends	**degli amici** m **/delle amiche** f _deh_•llyee ah•_mee_•chee/_dehl_•leh ah•_mee_•keh
a colleague	**un** m **/una** f collega oon/_oo_•nah kohl•_leh_•gah
colleagues	**dei colleghi** m **/delle colleghe** f day kohl•_leh_•ghee/ _deh_•leh kohl•_leh_•gheh
When's your birthday?	**Quando è il suo compleanno?** _kwahn_•doh eh eel _soo_•oh kohm•pleh•_ahn_•noh
How old are you?	**Quanti anni ha?** _kwahn_•tee _ahn_•nee ah
I'm...years old.	**Ho...anni.** oh...ahn•nee
Are you married?	**È sposato** m **/sposata** f**?** eh spoh•_zah_•toh/ spoh•_zah_•tah
I'm...	**Sono...** _soh_•noh...
single	**single** _seen_•guhl
engaged	**fidanzato** m **/ fidanzata** f fee•dan•_zah_•toh/ fee•dan•_zah_•tah/
married	**sposato** m **/sposata** f spoh•_zah_•toh/spoh•_zah_•tah
divorced	**divorziato** m **/divorziata** f dee•vohr•_tsyah_•toh/ dee•vohr•_tsyah_•tah
separated	**separato** m **/separata** f seh•pah•_rah_•toh/ seh•pah•_rah_•tah
widowed	**vedovo** m **/vedova** f _veh_•doh•voh/_veh_•doh•vah

A handshake is a common gesture among strangers or in formal settings. Traditionally, it is expected that a woman be the first to offer her hand. A kiss on both cheeks is used among friends and relatives. A nod and a smile suffice when greeting members of a group of people.

I have a boyfriend/girlfriend.	**Ho un ragazzo/una ragazza.**	oh oon rah·*gah*·tsoh/*oo*·nah rah·*gah*·tsah
Do you have children/grandchildren?	**Ha figli/nipoti?**	ah *fee*·llyee/nee·*poh*·tee

For Numbers, see page 167.

Work & School

What do you do for a living?	**Cosa fa?**	*koh*·zah fah
What are you studying?	**Cosa studia?**	*koh*·zah *stoo*·dyah
I'm studying Italian.	**Studio italiano.**	*stoo*·dyoh ee·tah·*lyah*·noh
I...	**Io...**	*ee*·oh...
work full-time/part-time	**lavoro full-time/part-time**	lah·*voh*·roh *fool*·tym/*pahrt*·tym
am unemployed	**sono disoccupato** *m* **/disoccupata** *f*	*soh*·noh dee·zohk·koo·*pah*·toh/dee·zohk·koo·*pah*·tah
work at home	**lavoro a casa**	lah·*voh*·roh ah *kah*·zah
Who do you work for?	**Per chi lavora?**	pehr kee lah·*voh*·rah
I work for...	**Lavoro per...**	lah·*voh*·roh pehr...
Here's my business card.	**Ecco il mio biglietto da visita.**	*ehk*·koh eel *mee*·oh bee·*llyeht*·toh dah *vee*·zee·tah

For Business Travel, see page 141.

Weather

What's the forecast?	**Come sono le previsioni?** _koh_•meh _soh_•noh leh preh•vee•_zyoh_•nee
What beautiful/ terrible weather!	**Che bel/brutto tempo!** keh behl/_broot_•toh _tehm_•poh
It's...	**Fa...** fah...
cool/warm.	**fresco/caldo.** _freh_•skoh/_kahl_•doh
It's cold/hot.	**freddo/caldo.** fah _frehd_•doh/_kahl_•doh
It's rainy.	**Piove.** _pyoh_•veh
It's sunny.	**C'è il sole.** cheh eel _soh_•leh
It's snowy.	**Nevica.** _neh_•vee•kah
It's icy.	**Gela.** _jeh_•lah
Do I need a jacket/an umbrella?	**Devo prendere una giacca/un ombrello?** deh•voh _prehn_•deh•reh _oo_•nah _jyahk_•kah/ oon ohm•_brehl_•loh

For Temperature, see page 173.

Romance

ESSENTIAL

Would you like to go out for a drink/dinner?	**Le va di andare a bere qualcosa/cena?** *leh vah dee ahn-<u>dah</u>-reh ah <u>beh</u>-reh kwahl-<u>koh</u>-zah/ <u>cheh</u>-nah*
What are your plans for tonight/ tomorrow?	**Che programmi ha per stasera/domani?** *keh proh-<u>grahm</u>-mee ah pehr stah-<u>seh</u>-rah/ doh-<u>mah</u>-nee*
Can I have your number?	**Mi dà il suo numero?** *mee dah eel <u>soo</u>-oh <u>noo</u>-meh-roh*
Can I buy you a drink?	**Posso offrirle qualcosa?** *<u>pohs</u>-soh ohf-<u>freer</u>-leh kwahl-<u>koh</u>-zah*
I like you.	**Mi piaci.** *mee <u>pyah</u>-chee*
I love you.	**Ti amo.** *tee <u>ah</u>-moh*

The Dating Game

Would you like to go out for a coffee/drink?	**Le va di andare a prendere un caffè/ bicchierino?** *leh vah dee ahn-<u>dah</u>-reh ah <u>prehn</u>-deh-reh oon kahf-<u>feh</u>/ bee-kyeh-<u>ree</u>-noh*
Would you like to go to dinner?	**Le va di andare a cena?** *leh vah dee ahn-<u>dah</u>-reh ah <u>cheh</u>-nah*
What are your plans for...?	**Che programmi ha per...?** *keh proh-<u>grahm</u>-mee ah pehr...*
today	**oggi** *<u>oh</u>-dgee*
tonight	**stasera** *stah-<u>seh</u>-rah*
tomorrow	**domani** *doh-<u>mah</u>-nee*
this weekend	**questo weekend** *<u>kweh</u>-stoh week-<u>ehnd</u>*

Where would you like to go?	**Dove le va di andare?** _doh_•veh leh vah dee ahn•_dah_•reh
I'd like to go to...	**Vorrei andare a...** vohr•_ray_ ahn•_dah_•reh ah...
Do you like...?	**Le piace...?** leh _pyah_•cheh...
Can I have your number/e-mail?	**Mi dà il suo numero/la sua e-mail?** mee dah eel _soo_•oh _noo_•meh•roh/lah _soo_•ah _ee_•mayl
Are you on Facebook/ Twitter?	**È su Facebook/Twitter?** eh soo feh•eez•book/ tweet•tehr
Can I join you?	**Mi posso sedere?** mee pohs•soh seh•_deh_•reh
You're very attractive.	**È molto attraente.** eh _mohl_•toh aht•trah•_ehn_•teh
Let's go somewhere quieter.	**Andiamo in un posto più tranquillo.** ahn•_dyah_•moh een oon _poh_•stoh pyoo trahn•_kweel_•loh

For Communications, see page 47.

Accepting & Rejecting

I'd love to.	**Mi piacerebbe moltissimo.** mee pyah•cheh•_rehb_•beh mohl•_tees_•see•moh
Where should we meet?	**Dove ci vediamo?** _doh_•veh chee veh•_dyah_•moh
I'll meet you at the bar/your hotel.	**Vediamoci al bar/nel suo hotel.** veh•_dyah_•moh•chee ahl bahr/nehl _soo_•oh oh•_tehl_
I'll come by at...	**Passo alle...** _pahs_•soh _ahl_•leh...
What is your address?	**Mi dà il suo indirizzo?** mee dah eel _soo_•oh een•dee•_ree_•tsoh
I'm busy.	**Ho da fare.** oh dah _fah_•reh
I'm not interested.	**Non m'interessa.** nohn meen•teh•_rehs_•sah
Leave me alone.	**Mi lasci in pace.** mee _lah_•shee een _pah_•cheh
Stop bothering me!	**Smetta d'infastidirmi!** _smeht_•tah deen•_fah_•stee•_deer_•mee

For Time, see page 169

Getting Intimate

Can I hug you/ kiss you?	**Posso abbracciarti/baciarti?** _pohs_•soh ahb•brah•_chyahr_•tee/bah•_chyahr_•tee
Yes.	**Sì.** _see_
No.	**No.** _noh_
Stop!	**Basta!** _bah_•stah
I like you.	**Mi piaci.** _mee pyah_•chee
I love you.	**Ti amo.** _tee ah_•moh

Sexual Preferences

Are you gay?	**Sei gay?** _say gay_
I'm…	**Sono…** _soh_•noh…
heterosexual	**eterosessuale** _eh_•teh•roh•sehs•_swah_•leh
homosexual	**omosessuale** _oh_•moh•sehs•_swah_•leh
bisexual	**bisex** _bee_•_sehks_
Do you like men/ women?	**Ti piacciono gli uomini/le donne?** _tee pyah_•chyoh•noh llyee _woh_•mee•nee/leh _dohn_•neh

Leisure Time

Sightseeing

ESSENTIAL

Where's the tourist information office?	**Dov'è l'ufficio informazioni turistiche?** doh-*veh* loof-*fee*-chyoh een-fohr-mah-*tsyoh*-nee too-*ree*-stee-keh
What are the main sights?	**Cosa c'è da vedere?** *koh*-zah ceh dah veh-*deh*-reh
Do you offer tours in English?	**Ci sono visite guidate in inglese?** chee *soh*-noh *vee*-zee-teh gwee-*dah*-teh een een-*gleh*-zeh
Can I have a map/guide?	**Mi può dare una cartina/guida?** mee pwoh *dah*-reh *oo*-nah kahr-*tee*-nah/*gwee*-dah

Tourist Information

Do you have information on...?	**Avete informazioni su...?** ah-*veh*-teh een-fohr-mah-*tsyoh*-nee soo...
Can you recommend...?	**Può consigliarmi...?** pwoh kohn-see-*llyahr*-mee...
a bus tour	**una gita in pullman** *oo*-nah *jee*-tah een *pool*-mahn
an excursion to...	**un'escursione a...** oo-neh-skoor-*syoh*-neh ah...
a sightseeing tour	**una gita turistica** *oo*-nah *jee*-tah too-*ree*-stee-kah

---

L'ufficio informazioni turistiche (tourist information office) can be found in almost every town; some may be located at the airport or main train station. Get local events listings, maps, transportation schedules and more at any of these offices.

112

On Tour

I'd like to go on the excursion to...	**Vorrei partecipare alla gita per...** *vohr·ray pahr·teh·chee·pah·reh ahl·lah jee·tah pehr...*
When's the next tour?	**Quando è la prossima gita?** *kwahn·doh eh lah prohs·see·mah jee·tah*
Are there tours in English?	**Ci sono visite guidate in inglese?** *chee soh·noh vee·zee·teh gwee·dah·teh een een·gleh·zeh*
Is there an English guide book/audio guide?	**C'è una guida/un'audio guida in inglese?** *cheh oo·nah gwee·dah/oo·now·dyoh gwee·dah een een·gleh·zeh*
What time do we leave/return?	**A che ora si torna?** *ah keh oh·rah see tohr·nah*
We'd like to see...	**Vorremmo vedere...** *vohr·rehm·moh veh·deh·reh...*
Can we stop here...?	**Possiamo fermarci...?** *pohs·syah·moh fehr·mahr·chee...*
to take photos	**per fare qualche foto** *pehr fah·reh kwahl·keh foh·toh*
for souvenirs	**per comprare qualche souvenir** *pehr kohm·prah·reh kwahl·keh soo·veh·neer*
for the toilets	**per andare in bagno** *pehr ahn·dah·reh een bah·nyoh*
Is it disabled-accessible?	**È accessibile ai disabili?** *eh ah·chehs·see·bee·leh ah·ee dee·zah·bee·lee*

Seeing the Sights

Where is/Where are…?	**Dov'è/Dove sono…?** *doh·veh/doh·veh soh·noh…*
the battleground	**il campo di battaglia?** *eel kahm·poh dee baht·tah·llyah?*
the botanical garden	**il giardino botanico** *eel jyahr·dee·noh boh·tah·nee·koh* ✓
the castle	**il castello** *eel kah·stehl·loh* ✓
the downtown area	**il centro** *eel chehn·troh* ✓
the fountain	**la fontana** *lah fohn·tah·nah*
the library	**la biblioteca** *lah bee·blyoh·teh·kah*
the market	**il mercato** *eel mehr·kah·toh*
the museum	**il museo** *eel moo·zeh·oh*
the old town	**la città vecchia** *lah cheet·tah vehk·kyah*
the opera house	**il teatro dell'opera** *eel teh·ah·troh deh·loh·peh·rah*
the palace	**il palazzo** *eel pah·lah·tsoh*
the park	**il parco** *eel pahr·koh*
the ruins	**le rovine** *leh roh·vee·neh*
the shopping area	**i negozi** *ee neh·goh·tzee*
the town hall	**il comune** *eel koh·moo·neh*
the town square	**la piazza principale** *lah pyah·tsah preen·chee·pah·leh*
Can you show me on the map?	**Può indicarmelo sulla cartina?** *pwoh een·dee·kahr·meh·loh sool·lah kahr·tee·nah*
It's…	**È…** *eh…*
amazing	**meraviglioso** *meh·rah·vee·llyoh·zoh*
beautiful	**bellissimo** *behl·lees·see·moh*
boring	**noioso** *noh·yoh·zoh*
interesting	**interessante** *een·teh·rehs·sahn·teh*
magnificent	**magnifico** *mah·nyee·fee·koh*

romantic	**romantico** roh·_mahn_·tee·koh
strange	**strano** _strah_·noh
stunning	**fenomenale** feh·noh·meh·_nah_·leh
terrible	**terribile** tehr·_ree_·bee·leh
ugly	**brutto** _broot_·toh
I (don't) like it.	**(Non) Mi piace.** (nohn) mee _pyah_·cheh

For Asking Directions, see page 33.

Religious Sites

Where's…?	**Dov'è…?** doh·_veh_…
the cathedral	**la cattedrale** lah kaht·teh·_drah_·leh
the Catholic/ Protestant church	**la chiesa cattolica/protestante** lah _kyeh_·zah kaht·_toh_·lee·kah/proh·teh·_stahn_·teh
the mosque	**la moschea** lah moh·_skeh_·ah
the shrine	**il santuario** eel sahn·_twah_·ryoh
the synagogue	**la sinagoga** lah see·nah·_goh_·gah
the temple	**il tempio** eel _tehm_·pyoh
What time is the mass/service?	**A che ora è la messa/il servizio?** ah keh _oh_·rah eh lah _mehs_·sah/eel sehr·_vee_·tsyoh

Shopping

ESSENTIAL

Where's the market/ mall [shopping centre]?	**Dov'è il mercato/centro commerciale?** doh·_veh_ eel mehr·_kah_·toh/_chehn_·troh kohm·mehr·_chyah_·leh
I'm just looking.	**Sto solo guardando.** stoh _soh_·loh gwahr·_dahn_·doh
Can you help me?	**Può aiutarmi?** pwoh ah·yoo·_tahr_·mee
I'm being helped.	**Mi stanno servendo.** mee _stahn_·noh sehr·_vehn_·doh
How much?	**Quant'è?** kwahn·_teh_
That one, please.	**Quello, per favore.** _kwehl_·loh pehr fah·_voh_·reh
That's all.	**Basta così.** _bah_·stah koh·_zee_
Where can I pay?	**Dove posso pagare?** _doh_·veh pohs·soh pah·_gah_·reh
I'll pay in cash/ by credit card.	**Pago in contanti/con carta di credito.** _pah_·goh een kohn·_tahn_·tee/kohn _kahr_·tah dee _kreh_·dee·toh
A receipt, please.	**Una ricevuta, per favore.** _oo_·nah ree·cheh·_voo_·tah pehr fah·_voh_·reh

At the Shops

Where's…?	**Dov'è…?** doh·_veh_…
the antiques store	**un negozio di antiquariato** oon neh·_goh_·tsyoh dee ahn·tee·kwah·_ryah_·toh
the bakery	**una panetteria** oo·nah pah·neht·teh·_ree_·ah
the bank	**una banca** _oo_·nah _bahn_·kah
the bookstore	**una libreria** _oo_·nah lee·breh·_ree_·ah
the camera store	**un negozio di fotografia** oon neh·_goh_·tsyoh dee foh·toh·grah·_fee_·ah
the clothing store	**un negozio di abbigliamento** oon neh·_goh_·tsyoh dee ahb·bee·llyah·_mehn_·toh

the delicatessen	**un negozio di gastronomia** *oon neh•goh•tsyoh dee gahs•troh•noh•mee•ah*
the department store	**un grande magazzino** *oon grahn•deh mah•gah•dzee•noh*
the gift shop	**un negozio di oggettistica** *oon neh•goh•tsyoh dee oh•djeht•tee•stee•kah*
the health food store	**un'erboristeria** *oo•nehr•boh•ree•steh•ree•ah*
the jeweler	**una gioiellieria** *oo•nah jyoh•yehl•lyeh•ree•ah*
the liquor store [off-licence]	**un'enoteca** *oo•neh•noh•teh•kah*
the market	**un mercato** *oon mehr•kah•toh*
the music store	**il negozio di musica?** *eel neh•goh•tsyoh dee moo•see•kah?*
the pastry shop	**una pasticceria** *oo•nah pah•stee•cheh•ree•ah*
the pharmacy [chemist]	**una farmacia** *oo•nah fahr•mah•chee•ah*
the produce [grocery] store	**il fruttivendolo** *eel froot•tee•vehn•doh•loh*
the shoe store	**un negozio di calzature** *oon neh•goh•tsyoh dee kahl•tsah•too•reh*
the shopping mall [shopping centre]	**un centro commerciale** *oon chehn•troh kohm•mehr•chyah•leh*
the souvenir store	**un negozio di souvenir** *oon neh•goh•tsyoh dee soo•veh•neer*
the supermarket	**un supermercato** *oon soo•pehr•mehr•kah•toh*
the tobacconist	**un tabaccaio** *oon tah•bahk•kah•yoh*
the toy store	**un negozio di giocattoli** *oon neh•goh•tsyoh dee jyoh•kaht•toh•lee*

Ask an Assistant

When do you open/close?	**Quando aprite/chiudete?** _kwahn·doh ah·pree·teh/ kyoo·deh·teh_
Where is/Where are…?	**Dov'è/Dove sono…?** _doh·veh/doh·veh soh·noh…_
the cashier	**la cassa** _lah kahs·sah_
the escalator	**le scale mobili** _leh skah·leh moh·bee·lee_
the elevator [lift]	**l'ascensore** _lah·shehn·soh·reh_
the fitting room	**il camerino** _eel kah·meh·ree·noh_
the store directory	**la piantina del negozio** _lah pyahn·tee·nah dehl neh·goh·tsyoh_
Can you help me?	**Può aiutarmi?** _pwoh ah·yoo·tahr·mee_
I'm just looking.	**Sto solo guardando.** _stoh soh·loh gwahr·dahn·doh_
I'm being helped.	**Mi stanno servendo.** _mee stahn·noh sehr·vehn·doh_
Do you have…?	**Avete…?** _ah·veh·teh…_
Can you show me…?	**Può mostrarmi…?** _pwoh moh·strahr·mee_
Can you ship it/ wrap it?	**Può spedirlo/incartarlo?** _pwoh speh·deer·loh/ een·kahr·tahr·loh_
How much?	**Quant'è?** _kwahn·teh_
That's all.	**Basta così.** _bah·stah koh·zee_

For Clothing, see page 124.

Personal Preferences

I'd like something…	**Vorrei qualcosa…** *vohr•ray kwahl•koh•zah…*
cheap/expensive	**di più economico/caro** *dee pyoo eh•koh•noh•mee•koh/kah•roh*
larger/smaller	**di più grande/piccolo** *dee pyoo grahn•deh/ peek•koh•loh*
from this region	**di tipico di questa zona** *dee tee•pee•koh dee kweh•stah dzoh•nah*
Around…euros.	**Intorno ai…euro.** *een•tohr•noh ah•ee… eh•oo•roh*
Is it real?	**È vero?** *eh veh•roh*
Can you show me…?	**Mi fa vedere…?** *mee fah veh•deh•reh*
That's not quite what I want.	**Non è proprio quello che volevo.** *nohn eh proh•pryoh kwehl•loh keh voh•leh•voh*
No, I don't like it.	**No, non mi piace.** *noh nohn mee pyah•cheh*
It's too expensive.	**È troppo caro.** *eh trohp•poh kah•roh*
I have to think about it.	**Devo pensarci.** *deh•voh pehn•sahr•chee*
I'll take it.	**Lo prendo.** *loh prehn•doh*

YOU MAY SEE…

APERTO	open
CHIUSO	closed
ENTRATA	entrance
CAMERINO	fitting room
CASSA	cashier
SOLO CONTANTI	cash only
SI ACCETTANO CARTE DI CREDITO	credit cards accepted
ORARIO D'APERTURA	business hours
USCITA	exit

YOU MAY HEAR...

Posso aiutarla? _pohs·soh ah·yoo·tahr lah_   Can I help you?

Un momento. _oon moh·mehn·toh_   One moment.

Che cosa desidera? _keh koh·zah deh·zee·deh·rah_   What would you like?

Altro? _ahl·troh_   Anything else?

Paying & Bargaining

How much?	**Quant'è?** _kwahn·teh_
I'll pay...	**Pago...** _pah·goh..._
in cash	**in contanti** _een kohn·tahn·tee_
by credit card	**con carta di credito** _kohn kahr·tah dee kreh·dee·toh_
by travelers check [cheque]	**con un travel cheque** _kohn oon trah·vehl chehk_
Can I use...?	**Posso usare...?** _pohs·soh oo·zah·reh..._
this ATM/debit card	**questo bancomat** _kweh·stoh bahn·koh·maht_
this credit card	**questa carta di credito** _kweh·stah kahr·tah dee kreh·dee·toh_
this gift card	**questo buono** _kweh·stoh bwoh·noh_
this prepaid card	**questa carta prepagata** _kweh·stah kahr·tah preh·pah·gah·tah_

Cash is still the most widely used and preferred method of payment, followed by **bancomat** (ATM cards). Credit cards are widely accepted, especially for larger purchases. Traveler's checks are accepted at most establishments.

How do I use this machine?	**Come si usa questa macchina?** _koh_·meh see _oo_·zah _kweh_·stah _mahk_·kee·nah
How much is left on the card?	**Quanto credito c'è sulla carta?** _kwahn_·toh _kreh_·dee·toh cheh sool·lah _kahr_·tah
A receipt, please.	**Una ricevuta, per favore.** _oo_·nah ree·cheh·_voo_·tah pehr fah·_voh_·reh
I'll give you…	**Le posso dare…** leh _pohs_·soh _dah_·reh…
I have only…euros.	**Ho solo…euro.** oh _soh_·loh…_eh_·oo·roh
Is that your best price?	**È il prezzo migliore che può farmi?** eh eel _preh_·tsoh mee·_llyoh_·reh keh pwoh _fahr_·mee

121

YOU MAY HEAR…

Come preferisce pagare? _koh_·meh preh·feh·_ree_·sheh pah·_gah_·reh	How are you paying?
La sua carta di credito è stata rifiutata. lah _soo_·ah _kahr_·tah dee _kreh_·dee·toh eh _stah_·tah ree·fyoo·_tah_·tah	Your credit card has been declined.
Un documento, per favore. oon doh·koo·_mehn_·toh pehr fah·_voh_·reh	ID, please.
Non accettiamo carte di credito. nohn ah·cheht·_tyah_·moh _kahr_·teh dee _kreh_·dee·toh	We don't accept credit cards.
Solo contanti, per favore. _soh_·loh kohn·_tahn_·tee pehr fah·_voh_·reh	Cash only, please.
Non ha spiccioli/banconote più piccole? nohn ah _spee_·chyoh·lee/bahn·koh·_noh_·teh pyoo _peek_·koh·leh	Do you have change/small bills [notes]?
Grazie. _grah_·tsyeh	Thank you.
Buona giornata! _bwoh_·nah jyohr·_nah_·tah	Have a nice day!

| That's too much. | **È troppo.** eh _trohp_·poh |
| Can you give me a discount? | **Mi fa un po' di sconto?** mee fah oon poh dee _skohn_·toh |

For Numbers, see page 167.

Making a Complaint

This is broken.	**È rotto** m **/rotta** f eh roht·_toh_/roh·_tah_
I bought it yesterday.	**L'ho comprato** m **/comprata** f **ieri.** loh kohm·prah·_toh_/kohm·prah·_tah_ yeh·ree
I'd like...	**Vorrei...** vohr·_ray_...
to exchange this	**cambiarlo** m **/cambiarla** f kahm·_byahr_·loh/ kahm·_byahr_·lah
a refund	**un rimborso** oon reem·_bohr_·soh
to see the manager	**parlare con il responsabile** pahr·_lah_·reh kohn eel reh·spohn·_sah_·bee·leh

Services

Can you recommend...?	**Può consigliarmi...?** pwoh kohn·see·_llyahr_·mee...
a barber	**un barbiere** oon bahr·_byeh_·reh
a dry cleaner	**il lavasecco** eel lah·vah·_sehk_·koh
a hairstylist	**un parrucchiere** oon pahr·rook·_kyeh_·reh
a laundromat [launderette]	**una lavanderia a gettone** _oo_·nah lah·vahn·deh·_ree_·ah ah jeht·_toh_·neh
a nail salon	**un salone di bellezza** oon sah·_loh_·neh dee beh·_leh_·tsah
a spa	**una stazione termali** _oo_·nah stah·_tsyoh_·neh tehr·_mah_·lee
a travel agency	**un'agenzia di viaggi** oo·nah·jehn·_tsee_·ah dee _vyah_·djee
Can you...this?	**Mi può...questo** m **/questa** f? mee pwoh... _kweh_·stoh/_kweh_·stah
alter	**cambiare** kahm·_byah_·reh
clean	**pulire** poo·_lee_·reh

fix [mend]	**riparare** *ree·pah·rah·reh*
press	**stirare** *stee·rah·reh*
When will it be ready?	**Per quando è pronto m /pronta f?**
	pehr kwahn·doh eh prohn·toh/prohn·tah

Hair & Beauty

I'd like…	**Vorrei…** *vohr·ray…*
an appointment for today/ tomorrow	**un appuntamento per oggi/domani** *oon ahp·poon·tah·mehn·toh pehr oh·djee/doh·mah·nee*
some color/ highlights	**fare il colore/i colpi di sole** *fah·reh eel koh·loh·reh/ee kohl·pee dee soh·leh*
my hair styled/ blow-dried	**fare la piega/asciugare** *fah·reh lah pyeh·gah/ah·shoo·gah·reh*
a haircut	**fare il taglio** *fah·reh eel tah·llyoh*
an eyebrow/ bikini wax	**fare la ceretta all'inguine** *fah·reh lah cheh·reht·tah ahl·leen·gwee·neh*
a facial	**fare la pulizia del viso** *fah-reh lah poo·lee·tsee·ah dehl vee·soh*
a manicure/ pedicure	**fare un manicure/pedicure** *fah-reh oon mah·nee·koor·eh/peh·dee·koor·eh*
a massage	**fare un massaggio** *fah·reh oon mahs·sah·djoh*
a trim	**dare una spuntatina** *dah·reh oo·nah spoon·tah·tee·nah*
Not too short.	**Non troppo corti.** *nohn trohp·poh kohr·tee*
Shorter here.	**Più corti qui.** *pyoo kohr·tee kwee*
Do you offer…?	**Fate…?** *fah·teh…*
acupuncture	**l'agopuntura** *lah·goh·poon·too·rah*
aromatherapy	**l'aromaterapia** *lah·roh·mah·teh·rah·pee·ah*
oxygen treatment	**l'ossigeno terapia** *lohs·see·jeh·noh teh·rah·pee·ah*
Do you have a sauna?	**C'è la sauna?** *cheh lah sah·ow·nah*

Italy is well-known for its **stazioni termale** (spas), which can be found throughout the country. Many of these spas are located near thermal springs and offer medicinal treatments. Some are day spas and others are hotel spas, which may offer weekend packages. Tipping is optional, as service is usually included.

Antiques

How old is it?	**Di quando è?** *dee kwahn·doh eh*
Do you have anything from the...period?	**Avete qualcosa del periodo...?** *ah·veh·teh kwahl·koh·zah dehl peh·ryoh·doh...*
Do I have to fill out any forms?	**Devo riempire un modulo?** *deh·voh ree·ehm·pee·reh oon moh·doo·loh*
Is there a certificate of authenticity?	**Ha il certificato di autenticità?** *ah eel chehr·tee·fee·kah·toh dee ow·tehn·tee·chee·tah*

Clothing

I'd like...	**Vorrei...** *vohr·ray...*
Can I try this on?	**Posso provarlo?** *pohs·soh proh·vahr·loh*
It doesn't fit.	**Non mi va bene.** *nohn mee vah beh·neh*
It's too...	**È troppo...** *eh trohp·poh...*
big/small	**grande/piccolo** *grahn·deh/peek·koh·loh*
short/long	**corto/lungo** *kohr·toh/loon·goh*
tight/loose	**stretto/largo** *streht·toh/lahr·goh*
Do you have this in size...?	**Non c'è la taglia...?** *nohn cheh lah tah·llyah...*
Do you have this in a bigger/smaller size?	**Non c'è in una taglia più grande/piccola?** *nohn cheh een oo·nah tah·llyah pyoo grahn·deh/peek·koh·lah*

For Numbers, see page 167.

Colors

I'd like something...	**Vorrei qualcosa di...** *vohr•ray kwahl•koh•zah dee...*
beige	**beige** *beyj*
black	**nero** *neh•roh*
blue	**blu** *bloo*
brown	**marrone** *mahr•roh•neh*
green	**verde** *vehr•deh*
gray	**grigio** *gree•jyoh*
orange	**arancione** *ahr•ahn•chyoh•neh*
pink	**rosa** *roh•zah*
purple	**viola** *vyoh•lah*
red	**rosso** *rohs•soh*
white	**bianco** *byahn•koh*
yellow	**giallo** *jyahl•loh*

Clothes & Accessories

a backpack	**lo zaino** *loh dzah•ee•noh*
a belt	**la cintura** *lah cheen•too•rah*
a bikini	**il bikini** *eel bee•kee•nee*
a blouse	**la camicia** *lah kah•mee•chyah*
a bra	**il reggiseno** *eel reh•djee•seh•noh*
briefs [underpants]/ panties	**lo slip** *loh sleep*
a coat	**il cappotto** *eel kahp•poht•toh*
a dress	**il vestito da donna** *eel veh•stee•toh dah dohn•nah*
a hat	**il cappello** *eel kahp•pehl•loh*
a jacket	**la giacca** *lah jyahk•kah*
jeans	**i jeans** *ee jeenz*
pajamas	**il pigiama** *eel pee•jyah•mah*
pants [trousers]	**i pantaloni** *ee pahn•tah•loh•nee*
pantyhose [tights]	**il collant** *eel kohl•lant*

a purse [handbag]	**la borsa** *lah <u>bohr</u>•sah*
a raincoat	**l'impermeabile** *leem•pehr•meh•<u>ah</u>•bee•leh*
a scarf	**la sciarpa** *lah <u>shahr</u>•pah*
a shirt	**la camicia** *lah kah•<u>mee</u>•chyah*
shorts	**i pantaloncini** *ee pahn•tah•lohn•<u>chee</u>•nee*
a skirt	**la gonna** *lah <u>gohn</u>•nah*
socks	**i calzini** *ee kahl•<u>tsee</u>•nee*
a suit	**l'abito** *<u>lah</u>•bee•toh*
sunglasses	**gli occhiali da sole** *llyee ohk•<u>kyah</u>•lee dah <u>soh</u>•leh*
a sweater	**il maglione** *eel mah•<u>llyoh</u>•neh*
a sweatshirt	**la felpa** *lah <u>fehl</u>•pah*
a swimsuit	**il costume da bagno** *eel koh•<u>stoo</u>•meh dah <u>bah</u>•nyoh*
a T-shirt	**la maglietta** *lah mah•<u>llyeht</u>•tah*
a tie	**la cravatta** *lah krah•<u>vaht</u>•tah*
underwear	**la biancheria intima** *lah byahn•keh•<u>ree</u>•ah <u>een</u>•tee•mah*

YOU MAY SEE...

UOMO	men's
DONNA	women's
BAMBINO	children's

Fabric

I'd like...	**Lo m /La f vorrei di...** *loh/lah vohr·ray dee...*
cotton	**cotone** *koh·toh·neh*
denim	**jeans** *jeenz*
lace	**pizzo** *pee·tsoh*
leather	**pelle** *pehl·leh*
linen	**lino** *lee·noh*
silk	**seta** *seh·tah*
wool	**lana** *lah·nah*
Is it machine washable?	**Si può lavare in lavatrice?** *see pwoh lah·vah·reh een lah·vah·tree·cheh*

Shoes

I'd like a pair of...	**Vorrei un paio di...** *vohr·ray oon pah·yoh dee...*
high-heels/flats	**scarpe col tacco alto/scarpe basse** *skahr·peh kohl tahk·koh ahl·toh/skahr·peh bahs·seh*
boots	**stivali** *stee·vah·lee*
loafers	**mocassini** *moh·kahs·see·nee*
sandals	**sandali** *sahn·dah·lee*
shoes	**scarpe** *skahr·peh*
slippers	**le ciabatte** *leh chah·baht·teh*
sneakers	**scarpe da tennis** *skahr·peh dah tehn·nees*
In size...	**Numero...** *noo·meh·roh...*

For Numbers, see page 167.

Sizes

small (S)	**piccola/S** *pee·koh·lah/ehs·seh*
medium (M)	**media/M** *meh·dyah/ehm·meh*
large (L)	**grande/L** *grahn·deh/ehl·leh*
extra large (XL)	**extra large/XL** *ehk·strah lahrj/ehks·ehl*
petite	**piccola** *peehk·koh·lah*
plus size	**taglia forte** *tah·llyah fohr·teh*

127

Newsstand & Tobacconist

Do you sell English-language newspapers?	**Avete qualche giornale in inglese?** *ah·veh·teh kwahl·keh jyohr·nah·leh een een·gleh·zeh*
I'd like…	**Vorrei…** *vohr·ray…*
candy [sweets]	**delle caramelle** *dehl·leh kah·rah·mehl·leh*
chewing gum	**della gomma da masticare** *dehl·lah gohm·mah dah mah·stee·kah·reh*
a chocolate bar	**del cioccolato** *dehl chyohk·koh·lah·toh*
a cigar	**un sigaro** *oon see·gah·roh*
a pack/carton of cigarettes	**un pacchetto/una stecca di sigarette** *oon pahk·keht·toh/oo·nah stehk·kah dee see·gah·reht·teh*
a lighter	**un accendino** *oon·ah·chehn·dee·noh*
a magazine	**una rivista** *oo·nah ree·vee·stah*
matches	**dei fiammiferi** *day fyahm·mee·feh·ree*
a newspaper	**un giornale** *oon jyohr·nah·leh*
a pen	**una penna** *oo·nah pehn·nah*
a postcard	**una cartolina** *oo·nah kahr·toh·lee·nah*
a (road)/town map of…	**una cartina (stradale) di…** *oo·nah kahr·tee·nah (strah·dah·lee) dee…*
stamps	**dei francobolli** *day frahn·koh·bohl·lee*

Photography

I'd like a/an… camera.	**Vorrei una macchina fotografica…** *vohr·ray oo·nah mahk·kee·nah foh·toh·grah·fee·kah…*
automatic	**automatica** *ow·toh·mah·tee·kah*
digital	**digitale** *dee·jee·tah·leh*
disposable	**usa e getta** *oo·zah eh jeht·tah*
I'd like…	**Vorrei…** *vohr·ray…*
digital prints	**far stampare delle foto digitali** *fahr stahm·pah·reh dehl·leh foh·toh dee·jee·tah·lee*

English-language newspapers, magazines and books can usually be found at newsstands, especially at train stations and in airports.

Smoking is not allowed in any public facility (banks, offices, bars, cafes, restaurants, buses, trains, etc.). Be aware that 'No Smoking' signs are not posted but you will incur a high fine if caught smoking in any public indoor area.

a battery	**una batteria** _oo_•nah baht•teh•_ree_•ah	
a memory card	**una scheda memoria** _oo_•nah skeh•dah meh•_moh_•ryah	
Can I print digital photos here?	**Posso stampare foto digitali?** _pohs_•soh stahm•_pah_•reh _foh_•toh dee•jee•_tah_•lee	

Souvenirs

blown glass	**il vetro soffiato** eel _veh_•troh sohf•_fyah_•toh
bottle of wine	**la bottiglia di vino** lah boht•_tee_•llyah dee _vee_•noh
box of chocolates	**la scatola di cioccolatini** lah _skah_•toh•lah dee chyohk•koh•lah•_tee_•nee
wood carvings	**il legno intagliato** eel _leh_•nyoh een•tah•_llyah_•toh
crystal	**il cristallo** eel kree•_stahl_•loh
doll	**la bambola** lah _bahm_•boh•lah
key ring	**il portachiavi** eel pohr•tah•_kyah_•vee
lace	**il pizzo** eel _pee_•tsoh
postcard	**la cartolina** lah kahr•toh•_lee_•nah
pottery	**la ceramica** lah cheh•_rah_•mee•kah
T-shirt	**la maglietta** lah mah•_llyeht_•tah
toy	**il giocattolo** eel jyoh•_kaht_•toh•loh
Can I see…?	**Posso vedere…?** _pohs_•soh veh•_deh_•reh…
Is this real?	**È vero?** eh _veh_•roh

It's in the window/ display case.	**È in vetrina/nella vetrinetta.** *eh een veh·tree·nah/ nehl·lah veh·tree·neht·tah*
I'd like...	**Vorrei...** *vohr·ray...*
a battery	**una batteria** *oo·nah baht·teh·ree·ah*
a bracelet	**un braccialetto** *oon brah·chyah·leht·toh*
a brooch	**una spilla** *oo·nah speel·lah*
a clock	**un orologio** *oo·noh·roh·loh·jyoh*
earrings	**un paio di orecchini** *oon pah·yoh dee oh·rehk·kee·nee*
a necklace	**una collana** *oo·nah kohl·lah·nah*
a ring	**un anello** *oo·nah·nehl·loh*
a watch	**un orologio** *oo·noh·roh·loh·jyoh*
I'd like...	**Lo m /La f vorrei...** *loh/lah vohr·ray...*
copper	**di rame** *dee rah·meh*
crystal	**in cristallo** *een kree·stahl·loh*
diamonds	**di diamanti** *dee dyah·mahn·tee*
white/yellow gold	**d'oro bianco/giallo** *doh·roh byahn·koh/jyahl·loh*
pearls	**di perle** *dee pehr·leh*
pewter	**di peltro** *dee pehl·troh*
platinum	**di platino** *dee plah·tee·noh*
sterling silver	**d'argento** *dahr·jehn·toh*
Can you engrave it?	**Potete fare un'incisione?** *poh·teh·teh fah·reh oo·neen·chee·zyoh·neh*

Italy offers an endless variety of handicrafts, from mouth-blown Murano glassware and delicate Capodimonte porcelain creations, to world-renowned fashion, antiques and of course gastronomic specialties. Traditional souvenirs are usually more expensive at souvenir shops. Local markets and small shops are also great places to find unique souvenirs.

Sport & Leisure

ESSENTIAL

When's the game?	**A che ora c'è la partita?** *ah keh oh•rah cheh lah pahr•tee•tah*
Where's…?	**Dov'è…?** *doh•veh…*
the beach	**la spiaggia** *lah spyah•djah*
the park	**il parco** *eel pahr•koh*
the pool	**la piscina** *lah pee•shee•nah*
Is it safe to swim here?	**Si può nuotare?** *see pwoh nwoh•tah•reh*
Can I hire golf clubs?	**Posso noleggiare delle mazze?** *pohs•soh noh•leh•djah•reh dehl•leh mah•tseh*
How much per hour?	**Qual è la tariffa per un'ora?** *kwah•leh lah tah•reef•fah pehr oo•noh•rah*
How far is it to…?	**Quanto dista a…?** *kwahn•toh dee•stah ah…*
Can you show me on the map?	**Può indicarmelo sulla cartina?** *pwoh een•dee•kahr•meh•loh sool•lah kahr•tee•nah*

Il calcio (soccer) is Italy's most popular year-round sport. Skiing and snowboarding are favorite winter pastimes for Italians. During the summer, sailing, windsurfing, hiking, tennis, scuba-diving, hang-gliding—especially on Lake Garda—and swimming are enjoyed.

Watching Sport

When's...?	**A che ora c'è...?** *ah keh oh·rah cheh...*
the baseball game	**la partita di baseball** *lah pahr·tee·tah dee bays·bahl*
the basketball game	**la partita di basket** *lah pahr·tee·tah dee bahs·keht*
the boxing match	**l'incontro di boxe** *leen·kohn·troh dee boh·kseh*
the cricket game	**partita di cricket** *pahr·tee·tah dee kree·keht*
the cycling race	**la gara di ciclismo** *lah gah·rah dee chee·kleez·moh*
the golf game	**la partita di golf** *lah pahr·tee·tah dee gohlf*
the soccer [football] game	**la partita di calcio** *lah pahr·tee·tah dee kahl·chyoh*
the tennis match	**la partita di tennis** *lah pahr·tee·tah dee tehn·nees*
the volleyball game	**la partita di pallavolo** *lah pahr·tee·tah dee pahl·lah·voh·loh*
Who's playing?	**Chi gioca?** *kee jyoh·kah*
Where's the racetrack/stadium?	**Dov'è il circuito/lo stadio?** *doh·veh eel cheer·kwee·toh/loh stah·dyoh*
Where can I place a bet?	**Dove si fanno le scommesse?** *doh·veh see fahn·noh leh skohm·mehs·seh*

For Tickets, see page 19.

Playing Sport

Where is/Where are…?	**Dov'è/Dove sono…?**	doh•_veh_/_doh_•veh soh•noh…
the golf course	**il campo da golf**	eel _kahm_•poh dah gohlf
the gym	**la palestra**	lah pah•_leh_•strah
the park	**il parco**	eel _pahr_•koh
the tennis courts	**i campi da tennis**	ee _kahm_•pee dah _teh_•nees
How much…?	**Quant'è la tariffa per…?**	kwahn•_teh_ lah tah•_reef_•fah pehr…
per day	**un giorno**	oon _jyohr_•noh
per hour	**un'ora**	oon•_oh_•rah
per game	**una partita**	_oo_•nah pahr•_tee_•tah
per round	**un turno/round?**	oon toohr•noh/oon rah•uh•nd?
Can I hire…	**Posso noleggiare…**	_pohs_•soh noh•leh•_djah_•reh…
some golf clubs	**delle mazze**	_dehl_•leh _mah_•tseh
some equipment	**l'attrezzatura**	laht•treh•tsah•_too_•rah
a racket	**una racchetta**	_oo_•nah rahk•_keht_•tah

At the Beach/Pool

Where's the beach/pool?	**Dov'è la spiaggia/piscina?**	doh•_veh_ lah _spyah_•djah/pee•_shee_•nah
Is there…?	**C'è…?**	cheh…
a kiddie pool	**una piscina per bambini**	_oo_•nah pee•_shee_•nah pehr bahm•_bee_•nee
a indoor/outdoor pool	**una piscina interna/esterna**	_oo_•nah pee•_shee_•nah een•_tehr_•nah/eh•_stehr_•nah
a lifeguard	**il bagnino**	eel bah•_nyee_•noh
Is it safe to swim/dive?	**Si può nuotare/tuffarsi?**	see pwoh nwoh•_tah_•reh/toof•_fahr_•see
Is it safe for children?	**È per bambini?**	eh pehr bahm•_bee_•nee
I'd like to hire…	**Vorrei noleggiare…**	vohr•_ray_ noh•leh•_djah_•reh

a deck chair	**una sedia a sdraio** <u>oo</u>·nah <u>seh</u>·dyah ah <u>sdrah</u>·yoh
a jet ski	**un acquascooter** oon <u>ah</u>·kwah·<u>skoo</u>·tehr
diving equipment	**l'attrezzatura subacquea** laht·treh·tsah·<u>too</u>·rah soo·<u>bah</u>·kweh·ah
a motorboat	**un motoscafo** oon moh·toh·<u>skah</u>·foh
a rowboat	**una barca a remi** <u>oo</u>·nah <u>bahr</u>·kah ah <u>reh</u>·mee
snorkeling equipment	**una maschera e il boccaglio** <u>oo</u>·nah <u>mah</u>·skeh·rah eh eel bohk·<u>kah</u>·llyoh
a surfboard	**una tavola da surf** <u>oo</u>·nah <u>tah</u>·voh·lah dah soorf
a towel	**un asciugamano** oon ah·shyoo·gah·<u>mah</u>·noh
an umbrella	**un ombrellone** oon ohm·brehl·<u>loh</u>·neh
water skis	**sci nautici** shee <u>now</u>·tee·chee
a windsurfer	**un windsurf** oon <u>weend</u>·soorf
For…hours.	**Per…ore.** pehr…<u>oh</u>·reh

With 7,600 kilometers (4,722 miles) of coastline, Italy has beaches to suit all tastes and budgets. From exclusive Ligurian and Sardinian beaches to popular Versilian and Adriatic spots, the seaside is a favorite holiday destination for Italians. Privately managed beaches are usually well-kept and offer a variety of services for a daily fee.

YOU MAY SEE…

SKI LIFT	drag lift
FUNIVIA	cable car
SEGGIOVIA	chair lift
PRINCIPIANTE	novice
INTERMEDIO	intermediate
ESPERTO	expert
PISTA CHIUSA	trail [piste] closed

Winter Sports

A lift pass for a day/ five days, please	**Un lift pass per un giorno/cinque giorni, per favore.** *oon leeft pahs pehr oon jyohr•noh/ cheen•kweh jyohr•nee pehr fah•voh•reh*
I'd like to hire…	**Vorrei noleggiare…** *vohr•ray noh•leh•djah•reh…*
boots	**un paio di stivali** *oon pah•yoh dee stee•vah•lee*
a helmet	**un casco** *oon kah•skoh*
skis	**un paio di sci** *oon pah•yoh dee shee*
poles	**un paio di racchette da sci** *oon pah•yoh dee rahk•keht•teh dah shee*
a snowboard	**uno snowboard** *oo•noh snoh•bohrd*
snowshoes	**le scarpe da neve** *lah skahr•peh dah neh•veh*
These are too big/small.	**Sono troppo grandi/piccoli.** *soh•noh trohp•poh grahn•dee/peek•koh•lee*
Are there lessons?	**Si possono prendere lezioni?** *see pohs•soh•noh prehn•deh•reh leh•tsyoh•nee*
I'm a beginner.	**Sono principiante.** *soh•noh preen•chee•pyahn•teh*
I'm experienced.	**Sono esperto m /esperta f.** *soh•noh eh•spehr•toh/ eh•spehr•tah*
A trail [piste] map, please.	**Una cartina delle piste, per favore.** *oo•nah kahr•tee•nah dehl•leh pee•steh pehr fah•voh•reh*

Out in the Country

A map..., please.	**Una cartina..., per favore.** _oo·nah kahr·tee·nah... pehr fah·voh·reh_
of this region	**della regione** _dehl·lah reh·jyoh·neh_
of the walking routes	**dei sentieri pedonali** _day sehn·tyeh·ree peh·doh·nah·lee_
of the bike routes	**delle piste ciclabili** _dehl·leh pee·steh chee·klah·bee·lee_
of the trails	**dei sentieri** _day sehn·tyeh·ree_
Is it...?	**È...?** _eh..._
easy	**facile** _fah·chee·leh_
difficult	**difficile** _deef·fee·chee·leh_
far	**lontano** _lohn·tah·noh_
steep	**ripido** _ree·pee·doh_
How far is it to...?	**Quanto dista a...?** _kwahn·toh dee·stah ah..._
Can you show me on the map?	**Può indicarmelo sulla cartina?** _pwoh een·dee·kahr·meh·loh sool·lah kahr·tee·nah_
I'm lost.	**Mi sono perso _m_ /persa _f_.** _mee soh·noh pehr·soh/pehr·sah_
Where's...?	**Dov'è...?** _doh·veh..._
the bridge	**il ponte** _eel pohn·teh_
the cave	**la grotta** _lah groht·tah_
the desert	**il deserto?** _eel deh·sehr·toh?_
the farm	**la fattoria** _lah faht·toh·ree·ah_
the field	**il campo** _eel kahm·poh_
the forest	**la foresta** _lah foh·reh·stah_
the hill	**la collina** _lah kohl·lee·nah_
the lake	**il lago** _eel lah·goh_
the mountain	**la montagna** _lah mohn·tah·nyah_
the nature preserve	**la riserva naturale** _lah ree·sehr·vah nah·too·rah·leh_
the viewpoint	**il belvedere** _eel behl·veh·deh·reh_
the park	**il parco** _eel pahr·koh_

the path	**il sentiero** *eel sehn·tyeh·roh*
the peak	**il picco** *eel peek·koh*
the picnic area	**l'area picnic** *lah·reh·ah peek·neek*
the pond	**lo stagno** *loh stah·nyoh*
the river	**il fiume** *eel fyoo·meh*
the sea	**il mare** *eel mah·reh*
the (thermal) spring	**la sorgente (termale)** *lah sohr·jehn·teh (tehr·mah·leh)*
the stream	**il ruscello** *eel roo·shehl·loh*
the valley	**la valle** *lah vahl·leh*
the vineyard	**il vigneto** *eel vee·nyeh·toh*
the waterfall	**la cascata** *lah kah·skah·tah*

Going Out

ESSENTIAL

What's there to do at night?	**Cosa si fa di sera?** *koh·zah see fah dee seh·rah*
Do you have a program of events?	**Mi può dare un calendario degli eventi?** *mee pwoh dah·reh oon kah·lehn·dah·ryoh deh·llyee eh·vehn·tee*
What's playing tonight?	**Cosa c'è in programma stasera?** *koh·zah cheh een proh·grahm·mah stah·seh·rah*
Where's...?	**Dov'è...?** *doh·veh...*
the downtown area	**il centro** *eel chehn·troh*
the bar	**il bar** *eel bahr*
the dance club	**la discoteca** *lah dee·skoh·teh·kah*
Is there a cover charge?	**C'è un costo aggiuntivo?** *cheh oon koh·stoh ah·djoon·tee·voh*

Entertainment

Can you recommend…?	**Può consigliarmi…?** *pwoh kohn•see•llyahr•mee…*
a concert	**un concerto** *oon kohn•chehr•toh*
a movie	**un film** *oon feelm*
an opera	**un'opera** *oo•noh•peh•rah*
a play	**una rappresentazione teatrale** *oo•nah rahp•preh•zehn•tah•tsyoh•neh teh•ah•trah•leh*
When does it start/end?	**Quando inizia/finisce?** *kwahn•doh ee•nee•tsyah/fee•nee•sheh*
What's the dress code?	**Come ci si deve vestire?** *koh•meh chee see deh•veh veh•stee•reh*
I like…	**Mi piace…** *mee pyah•cheh…*
classical music	**la musica classica** *lah moo•zee•kah klah•see•kah*
folk music	**la musica folk** *lah moo•zee•kah fohlk*

YOU MAY HEAR…

Spegnere il cellulare, per favore. *speh•nyeh•reh eel chehl•loo•lah•reh pehr fah•voh•reh* Turn off your cell [mobile] phones, please.

A calendar of events may be found at local tourist information offices or on the venues' websites. Local events are often posted around town, so be sure to stop and read the posters. The hotel concierge is also a good source for local information.

jazz	**il jazz** *eel jahz*
pop music	**la musica pop** *lah moo·zee·kah pohp*
rap	**il rap** *eel rahp*

For Tickets, see page 19.

Nightlife

What's there to do at night?	**Cosa si fa di sera?** *koh·zah see fah dee seh·rah*
Can you recommend...?	**Può consigliarmi...?** *pwoh kohn·see·llyahr·mee...*
a bar	**un bar** *oon bahr*
a casino	**un casinò** *oon kah·zee·noh*
a dance club	**una discoteca** *oo·nah dee·skoh·teh·kah*
a gay club	**un locale gay** *oon loh·kah·leh gay*
a jazz club	**un locale jazz** *oon loh·kah·leh jahz*
a club with Italian music	**un locale con musica italiana** *oon loh·kah·leh kohn moo·zee·kah ee·tah·lyah·nah*
Is there live music?	**C'è musica dal vivo?** *cheh moo·zee·kah dahl vee·voh*
How do I get there?	**Come ci si arriva?** *koh·meh chee see ahr·ree·vah*
Is there a cover charge?	**C'è un costo aggiuntivo?** *cheh oon koh·stoh ah·djoon·tee·voh*
Let's go dancing.	**Andiamo a ballare.** *ahn·dyah·moh ah bahl·lah·reh*
Is this area safe at night?	**Questa zona è sicura di notte?** *Kweh·stah·dzoh·nah eh see·koo·rah dee noht·teh?*

Special
Requirements

Business Travel

ESSENTIAL

I'm here on business.	**Sono qui per lavoro.** <u>soh</u>•noh kwee pehr lah•<u>voh</u>•roh
Here's my business card.	**Ecco il mio biglietto da visita.** <u>ehk</u>•koh eel <u>mee</u>•oh bee•<u>llyeht</u>•toh dah <u>vee</u>•zee•tah
Can I have your card?	**Mi può dare il suo biglietto da visita?** mee pwoh <u>dah</u>•reh eel <u>soo</u>•oh bee•<u>llyeht</u>•toh dah <u>vee</u>•zee•tah
I have a meeting with...	**Ho una riunione con...** oh <u>oo</u>•nah ryoo•<u>nyoh</u>•neh kohn...
Where's...?	**Dov'è...?** doh•<u>veh</u>...
the business center	**il centro business** eel <u>chehn</u>•troh <u>bees</u>•nehs
the convention hall	**la sala congressi** lah <u>sah</u>•lah kohn•<u>grehs</u>•see
the meeting room	**la sala meeting** lah <u>sah</u>•lah <u>mee</u>•teeng

141

> **Buongiorno** (good morning) or **buonasera** (good afternoon/evening) are suitable greetings in business situations, and are often accompanied by a handshake. **Piacere** (pleased to meet you) is a polite response at introductions. When saying goodbye to business acquaintances, it is polite to use the formal **arrivederla**.

On Business

I'm here for...	**Sono qui per...** <u>soh</u>•noh kwee pehr...
a seminar	**un seminario** oon seh•mee•<u>nah</u>•ryoh
a conference	**una conferenza** <u>oo</u>•nah kohn•feh•<u>rehn</u>•tsah
a meeting	**una riunione** <u>oo</u>•nah ryoo•<u>nyoh</u>•neh

142

My name is…	**Mi chiamo…** *mee kyah•moh…*
May I introduce my colleague…	**Le presento il mio collega** *m* /**la mia collega** *f*…
	leh preh•zehn•toh eel mee•oh kohl•leh•gah/ lah mee•ah kohl•leh•gah…
I have a meeting/ an appointment with…	**Ho una riunione/un appuntamento con…**
	oh oo•nah ryoo•nyoh•neh/oon ahp•poon•tah•mehn•toh kohn…
I'm sorry I'm late.	**Scusi il ritardo.** *skoo•see eel ree•tahr•doh*
I need an interpreter.	**Mi serve un interprete.** *mee sehr•veh oon een•tehr•preh•teh*
You can contact me at the…Hotel.	**Sono raggiungibile all'hotel…** *soh•noh rah•djoon•jee•bee•leh ahl•loh•tehl…*

YOU MAY HEAR…

Ha un appuntamento?	Do you have an
ah oon ahp•poon•tah•mehn•toh	appointment?
Con chi? *kohn kee*	With whom?
Il signor *m* /**La signora** *f* **è in riunione.**	He/She is in a
eel see•nyohr/lah see•nyoh•rah eh een ryoo•nyoh•neh	meeting.
Un momento, per favore.	One moment,
oon moh•mehn•toh pehr fah•voh•reh	please.
Si accomodi. *see ahk•koh•moh•dee*	Have a seat.
Desidera qualcosa da bere?	Would you like
deh•zee•deh•rah kwahl•koh•zah dah beh•reh	something to drink?
Grazie per essere venuto *m* /**venuta** *f*.	Thank you for
grah•tsyeh pehr eh•seh•reh veh•noo•toh/ veh•noo•tah	coming.

I'm here until...	**Sono qui fino a...** _soh_·noh kwee _fee_·noh ah...	
I need to...	**Ho bisogno di...** oh bee·_soh_·nyoh dee...	
make a call	**fare una telefonata** _fah_·reh _oo_·nah teh·leh·foh·_nah_·tah	
make a photocopy	**fare una fotocopia** _fah_·reh _oo_·nah foh·toh·_koh_·pyah	
send an e-mail	**inviare un'e-mail** een·_vyah_·reh oon _ee_·mayl	
send a fax	**inviare un fax** een·_vyah_·reh oon fahks	
send a package (for next-day delivery)	**inviare un pacco (da un giorno all'altro)** een·_vyah_·reh oon _pahk_·koh (dah oon _jyohr_·noh ahl·_lahl_·troh)	
It was a pleasure to meet you.	**È stato un piacere.** eh _stah_·toh oon pyah·_cheh_·reh	

For Communications, see page 47.

Traveling with Children

ESSENTIAL

Is there a discount for kids?	**È previsto uno sconto per bambini?** eh preh·_vee_·stoh _oo_·noh _skohn_·toh pehr bahm·_bee_·nee
Can you recommend a babysitter?	**Può consigliarmi una babysitter?** pwoh kohn·see·_llyahr_·mee _oo_·nah bah·bee·_seet_·tehr
Do you have a child's seat/highchair?	**Avete un seggiolino/seggiolone per bambini?** ah·_veh_·teh oon seh·djoh·_lee_·noh/seh·djoh·_loh_·neh pehr bahm·_bee_·nee
Where can I change the baby?	**Dove posso cambiare il bambino?** _doh_·veh _poh_·soh kahm·_byah_·reh eel bahm·_bee_·noh

Out & About

Can you recommend something for kids?	**Può consigliarmi qualcosa per i bambini?** *pwoh kohn·see·llyahr·mee kwahl·koh·zah pehr ee bahm·bee·nee*
Where's…?	**Dov'è…?** *doh·veh…*
the amusement park	**il luna park** *eel loo·nah pahrk*
the arcade	**il parco videogiochi** *eel pahr·koh vee·deh·oh·jyoh·kee*
the kiddie [paddling] pool	**la piscina per bambini** *lah pee·shee·nah pehr bahm·bee·nee*
the park	**il parco** *eel pahr·koh*
the playground	**il parco giochi** *eel pahr·koh jyoh·kee*
the zoo	**lo zoo** *loh dzooh*
Are kids allowed?	**Si possono portare i bambini?** *see pohs·soh·noh pohr·tah·reh ee bahm·bee·nee*
Is it safe for kids?	**È per bambini?** *eh pehr bahm·bee·nee*
Is it suitable for… year olds?	**È adatto ai bambini di…anni?** *eh ah·daht·toh ah·ee bahm·bee·nee dee…ahn·nee*

For Numbers, see page 167.

YOU MAY HEAR...

Che carino m/carina f!
keh kah·ree·noh/kah·ree·nah

How cute!

Come si chiama? *koh·meh see kyah·mah*

What's his/her name?

Quanti anni ha? *kwahn·tee ahn·nee ah*

How old is he/she?

Baby Essentials

Do you have...?	**Avete...?** *ah·veh·teh...*
a baby bottle	**un biberon** *oon bee·beh·rohn*
baby food	**del cibo per neonati** *dehl chee·boh pehr neh·oh·nah·tee*
baby wipes	**delle salviette per neonati** *dehl·leh sahl·vyeht·teh pehr neh·oh·nah·tee*
a car seat	**un seggiolino per auto** *oon seh·djoh·lee·noh pehr ow·toh*
a children's menu/portion	**il menù/le porzioni per bambini** *eel meh·noo/leh pohr·tsyoh·nee pehr bahm·bee·nee*
a child's seat/ highchair	**un seggiolino/seggiolone per bambini** *oon seh·djoh·lee·noh/seh·djoh·loh·neh pehr bahm·bee·nee*
a crib/cot	**una culla/un lettino** *oo·nah kool·lah/ oon leht·tee·noh*
diapers [nappies]	**dei pannolini** *day pahn·noh·lee·nee*
formula [baby food]	**del latte in polvere** *dehl laht·teh een pohl·veh·reh*
a pacifier [dummy]	**un ciucciotto** *oon chyoo·chyoht·toh*
a playpen	**un box** *oon bohks*
a stroller [pushchair]	**un passeggino** *oon pah·seh·djee·noh*

| Can I breastfeed the baby here? | **Posso allattare il bambino?** _poh_•soh _ahl_•laht•_tah_•reh eel bahm•_bee_•noh |
| Where can I breastfeed/change the baby? | **Dove posso allattare/cambiare il bambino?** _doh_•veh _poh_•soh ahl•laht•_tah_•reh/ kahm•_byah_•reh eel bahm•_bee_•noh |

For Dining with Children, see page 63.

Babysitting

Can you recommend a babysitter?	**Può consigliarmi una babysitter?** pwoh kohn•see•_llyahr_•mee _oo_•nah bah•bee•_seet_•tehr
What do you/they charge?	**Quanto si paga?** _kwahn_•toh see _pah_•gah
I'll be back at...	**Torno per le...** _tohr_•noh pehr leh...
If you need to contact me, call...	**Mi potete trovare al numero...** mee poh•_tay_•teh troh•_vahr_•eh ahl _noo_•meh•roh...

For Numbers, see page 167.

For Time, see page 169.

Health & Emergency

| Can you recommend a pediatrician? | **Può consigliarmi un pediatra?** pwoh kohn•see•_llyahr_•mee oon peh•_dyah_•trah |

My son/daughter is allergic to…	**Il mio bambino/La mia bambina è allergico m/ allergica f a…** *eel mee-oh bahm-bee-noh/lah mee-ah bahm-bee-nah eh ahl-lehr-jee-koh/ahl-lehr-jee-kah ah…*
My son/daughter is missing.	**Il mio bambino m/La mia bambina f è scomparso m/scomparsa f.** *eel mee-oh bahm-bee-noh/lah mee-ah bahm-bee-nah eh skohm-pahr-soh/skohm-pahr-sah*
Have you seen a boy/girl?	**Ha visto un bambino m /una bambina f?** *ah vee-stoh oon bahm-bee-noh/oo-nah bahm-bee-nah*

For Meals & Cooking, see page 65.

For Health, see page 153.

For Police, see page 151.

Disabled Travelers

ESSENTIAL

Is there…?	**C'è…?** *cheh…*
access for the disabled	**l'accesso ai disabili** *lah-cheh-soh ah-ee dee-zah-bee-lee*
a wheelchair ramp	**la rampa per le sedie a rotelle** *lah rahm-pah pehr leh seh-dyeh ah roh-tehl-leh*
a disabled-accessible toilet	**la toilette per i disabili** *lah twah-leht pehr ee dee-zah-bee-lee*
I need…	**Mi serve…** *mee sehr-veh…*
assistance	**assistenza** *ah-see-stehn-tsah*
an elevator [a lift]	**un ascensore** *oon ah-shehn-soh-reh*
a ground-floor room	**una stanza al pianterreno** *oo-nah stahn-tsah ahl pyahn-tehr-reh-noh*

Asking for Assistance

I'm...	**Sono...** _soh•noh..._
disabled	**disabile** _dee•zah•bee•leh_
visually impaired	**ipovedente** _ee•poh•veh•dehn•the_
deaf	**sordo** _sohr•doh_
hearing impaired	**audioleso** _ow•dyoh•leh•soh_
I cannot walk far/ use the stairs.	**Non posso camminare tanto/fare le scale.** _nohn poh•soh kahm•mee•nah•reh tahn•toh/ fah•reh leh skah•leh_
Can I bring my wheelchair?	**Posso portare la sedia a rotelle?** _poh•soh pohr•tah•reh lah seh•dyah ah roh•tehl•leh_
Are guide dogs permitted?	**I cani guida sono permessi?** _ee kah•nee gwee•dah soh•noh pehr•meh•see_
Can you help me?	**Può aiutarmi?** _pwoh ah•yoo•tahr•mee_
Please open/hold the door.	**Per favore, potrebbe aprire/tenere aperta la porta.** _pehr fah•voh•reh poh•trehb•beh ah•pree•reh/ teh•neh•reh ah•pehr•tah lah pohr•tah_

In an Emergency

Emergencies

ESSENTIAL

Help!	**Aiuto!** ah•yoo•toh	
Go away!	**Se ne vada!** seh neh vah•dah	
Stop, thief!	**Fermi, al ladro!** fehr•mee ahl lah•droh	
Get a doctor!	**Un medico!** oon meh•dee•koh	
Fire!	**Al fuoco!** ahl fwoh•koh	
I'm lost.	**Mi sono perso m /persa f.** mee soh•noh pehr•soh/pehr•sah	
Can you help me?	**Può aiutarmi?** pwoh ah•yoo•tahr•mee	

In an emergency, dial: **112** for the police
115 for the fire brigade
118 for the ambulance.

YOU MAY HEAR...

Riempia questo modulo. ree•ehm•pyah kweh•stoh moh•doo•loh
Fill out this form.

Un documento, per favore. oon doh•koo•mehn•toh pehr fah•voh•reh
Your identification, please.

Quando/Dove è successo? kwahn•doh/doh•veh eh soo•cheh•soh
When/Where did it happen?

Che aspetto aveva? keh ah•speht•toh ah•veh•vah
What does he/she look like?

Police

ESSENTIAL

Call the police!	**Chiami la polizia!** _kyah·mee lah poh·lee·tsee·ah_
Where's the police station?	**Dov'è il commissariato?** _doh·veh eel kohm·mee·sah·ryah·toh_
There was an accident/attack.	**C'è stato un incidente/stata un'aggressione.** _cheh stah·toh oon een·chee·dehn·teh/stah·tah oo·nahg·grehs·syoh·neh_
My son/daughter is missing.	**Il mio bambino _m_ /La mia bambina _f_ è scomparso _m_ /scomparsa _f_.** _eel mee·oh bahm·bee·noh/lah mee·ah bahm·bee·nah eh skohm·pahr·soh/skohm·pahr·sah_
I need an interpreter	**Ho bisogno di un interprete.** _oh bee·soh·nyoh dee oon een·tehr·preh·teh_
I'm innocent.	**Sono innocente.** _soh·noh een·noh·chehn·teh_
I need to contact my lawyer/make a phone call.	**Ho bisogno di chiamare il mio avvocato/ fare una telefonata.** _oh bee·soh·nyoh dee kyah·mah·reh eel mee·oh ahv·voh·kah·toh/ fah·reh oo·nah teh·leh·foh·nah·tah_

Crime & Lost Property

I'd like to report...	**Vorrei denunciare...** _vohr·ray deh·noon·chyah·reh..._
a mugging	**uno scippo** _oo·noh sheep·poh_
a rape	**uno stupro** _oo·noh stoo·proh_
a theft	**un furto** _oon foor·toh_
I've been mugged/ robbed.	**Mi hanno scippato/derubato.** _mee ahn·noh sheep·pah·toh/deh·roo·bah·toh_
I've lost my...	**Ho perso...** _oh pehr·soh..._

My...was stolen.	**Mi hanno rubato...** *mee ahn·noh roo·bah·toh*
backpack	**lo zaino** *loh dzah·ee·noh*
bicycle	**la bicicletta** *lah bee·chee·kleht·tah*
camera	**la macchina fotografica** *lah mahk·kee·nah foh·toh·grah·fee·kah*
computer	**il computer** *eel kohm·pyoo·tehr*
(hire) car	**l'auto a noleggio** *l·ow·toh ah noh·leh·djoh*
credit card	**la carta di credito** *lah kahr·tah dee kreh·dee·toh*
jewelry	**i gioielli** *ee joy·ehl·lee*
money	**il denaro** *eel deh·nah·roh*
passport	**il passaporto** *eel pahs·sah·pohr·toh*
purse [handbag]	**la borsa** *lah bohr·sah*
traveler's checks [cheques]	**i travelers cheques** *ee trah·vehl·lehrs chehks*
wallet	**il portafogli** *eel pohr·tah·foh·llyee*
I need a police report.	**Ho bisogno di un verbale.** *oh bee·soh·nyoh dee oon vehr·bah·leh*
Where is the British/ American/Irish embassy?	**Dove si trova l'ambasciata britannica/americana/ irlandese?** *Doh·veh see troh·vah l·ahm·bah·shah·tah bree·tahn·nee·kah/ah·meh·ree·kah·nah/eer·lahn·deh·seh?*

ESSENTIAL

I'm sick [ill].	**Sto male.** *stoh mah·leh*
I need an English-speaking doctor.	**Ho bisogno di un medico che parli inglese.** *oh bee·soh·nyoh dee oon meh·dee·koh keh pahr·lee een·gleh·zeh*
It hurts here.	**Mi fa male qui.** *mee fah mah·leh kwee*
I have a stomachache.	**Ho mal di stomaco.** *oh mahl dee stoh·mah·koh*

Finding a Doctor

Can you recommend a doctor/dentist?	**Mi può consigliare un medico/dentista?** *mee pwoo kohn·see·llyah·reh oon meh·dee·koh/dehn·tee·stah*
Can the doctor come here?	**Il medico può venire?** *eel meh·dee·koh pwoh veh·nee·reh*
I need an English-speaking doctor.	**Ho bisogno di un medico che parli inglese.** *oh bee·soh·nyoh dee oon meh·dee·koh keh pahr·lee een·gleh·zeh*
What are the office hours?	**Che orari fate?** *keh oh·rah·ree fah·teh*
I'd like an appointment for…	**Vorrei un appuntamento…** *vohr·ray oon ahp·poon·tah·mehn·toh…*
today	**per oggi** *pehr oh·djee*
tomorrow	**per domani** *pehr doh·mah·nee*
as soon as possible	**al più presto possibile** *ahl pyoo preh·stoh pohs·see·bee·leh*
It's urgent.	**È urgente.** *eh oor·jehn·teh*

Symptoms

I'm bleeding.	**Perdo sangue.** <u>pehr</u>•doh <u>sahn</u>•gweh
I'm constipated.	**Sono costipato.** <u>soh</u>•noh koh•stee•<u>pah</u>•toh
I'm dizzy.	**Mi gira la testa.** mee <u>jee</u>•rah lah <u>teh</u>•stah
I'm nauseous.	**Ho la nausea.** oh lah <u>now</u>•zeh•ah
I'm vomiting.	**Vomito.** <u>voh</u>•mee•toh
It hurts here.	**Mi fa male qui.** mee fah <u>mah</u>•leh kwee
I have…	**Ho…** oh…
an allergic reaction	**una reazione allergica** <u>oo</u>•nah reh•ah•<u>tsyoh</u>•neh ahl•<u>lehr</u>•jee•kah
chest pain	**un dolore al petto** oon doh•<u>loh</u>•reh ahl <u>peht</u>•toh
cramps	**crampi** krahm•pee
diarrhea	**la diarrea** lah dee•ahr•<u>reh</u>•ah
an earache	**mal d'orecchio** mahl doh•<u>rehk</u>•kyoh
a fever	**la febbre** lah <u>fehb</u>•breh
pain	**un dolore** oon doh•<u>loh</u>•reh
a rash	**un rossore** oon rohs•<u>soh</u>•reh
a sting	**una puntura** <u>oo</u>•nah poon•<u>too</u>•rah
a sprain	**una storta** <u>oo</u>•nah <u>stohr</u>•tah
some swelling	**un gonfiore** oon gohn•<u>fyoh</u>•reh
a sore throat	**il mal di gola** eel mahl dee <u>goh</u>•lah
a stomach ache	**mal di stomaco** mahl dee <u>stoh</u>•mah•koh
sunstroke	**l'insolazione** leen•soh•lah•<u>tsyoh</u>•neh
I've been sick [ill] for…days.	**Sto male da…giorni.** stoh <u>mah</u>•leh dah…<u>jyohr</u>•nee

Conditions

I'm...	**Sono...** _soh_·noh...	
anemic	**anemico** *m* /**anemica** *f* ah·_neh_·mee·koh/	
	ah·_neh_·mee·kah	
asthmatic	**asmatico** *m* /**asmatica** *f* ahz·_mah_·tee·koh/	
	ahz·_mah_·tee·kah	
diabetic	**diabetico** *m* /**diabetica** *f* dee·ah·_beh_·tee·koh/	
	dee·ah·_beh_·tee·kah	
epileptic	**epilettico** *m* /**epilettica** *f* eh·pee·leht·tee·koh/	
	eh·pee·leht·tee·kah	
I'm allergic to	**Sono allergico** *m* /**allergica** *f* **agli**	
antibiotics/	**antibiotici/alla penicillina.** _soh_·noh	
penicillin.	ahl·_lehr_·jee·koh/ahl·_lehr_·jee·kah _ah_·llyee	
	ahn·tee·_byoh_·tee·chee/_ahl_·lah peh·nee·cheel·_lee_·nah	
I have...	**Soffro di...** _sohf_·froh dee...	
arthritis	**artrite** ahr·_tree_·teh	
a heart condition	**cuore** _kwoh_·reh	
high/low blood	**alta/bassa pressione** _ahl_·tah/_bahs_·sah	
pressure	prehs·_syoh_·neh	
I'm on...	**Prendo...** _prehn_·doh...	

Treatment

Do I need a	**Ci vuole la ricetta?**
prescription/medicine?	chee vwoh·leh lah ree·cheht·tah?
Can you prescribe	**Mi può prescrivere un medicinale generico?**
a generic drug	mee pwoh preh·skree·veh·reh oon
[unbranded	meh·dee·chee·nah·leh jeh·neh·ree·koh
medication]?	
Where can I get it?	**Dove lo posso trovare?**
	doh·veh loh pohs·soh troh·vah·reh?

Hospital

Notify my family, please.	**Avvisi la mia famiglia, per favore.**
	ahv•vee•zee lah mee•ah fah•mee•llyah pehr fah•voh•reh
I'm in pain.	**Sto male.** *stoh mah•leh*
I need a doctor/nurse.	**Ho bisogno di un medico/un'infermiera.**
	oh bee•zoh•nyoh dee oon meh•dee•koh/ oo•neen•fehr•myeh•rah
When are visiting hours?	**Qual è l'orario delle visite?** *kwahl eh loh•rah•ryoh dehl•leh vee•zee•teh*
I'm visiting...	**Sto visitando...** *stoh vee•zee•tahn•doh...*

YOU MAY HEAR...

Cosa c'è che non va? *koh•zah cheh keh nohn vah*	What's wrong?
Dove le fa male? *doh•veh leh fah mah•leh*	Where does it hurt?
Fa male qui? *fah mah•leh kwee*	Does it hurt here?
Prende farmaci? *prehn•deh fahr•mah•chee*	Are you on medication?
Ha allergie? *ah ahl•lehr•jee•eh*	Are you allergic to anything?
Apra la bocca. *ah•prah lah bohk•kah*	Open your mouth.
Respiri profondamente. *reh•spee•ree proh•fohn•dah•mehn•teh*	Breathe deeply.
Vada in ospedale. *vah•dah een oh•speh•dah•leh*	Go to the hospital.
È... *eh...*	It's...
rotto *roht•toh*	broken
contagioso *kohn•tah•jyoh•zoh*	contagious
infetto *een•feht•toh*	infected
È una storta. *eh oo•nah stohr•tah*	It's sprained.
Niente di grave. *nyehn•teh dee grah•veh*	It's nothing serious.

157

Dentist

I have a broken tooth.	**Ho un dente rotto.** *oh oon <u>dehn</u>·teh <u>roht</u>·toh*
I have lost a filling.	**Ho perso un'otturazione.** *oh <u>pehr</u>·soh oo·noht·too·rah·<u>tsyoh</u>·neh*
I have a toothache.	**Ho mal di denti.** *oh mahl dee <u>dehn</u>·tee*
Can you fix this denture?	**Può aggiustare la dentiera?** *pwoh ah·djoo·<u>stah</u>·reh lah dehn·<u>tyeh</u>·rah*

Gynecologist

I have cramps/ a vaginal infection.	**Ho i crampi/un'infezione vaginale.** *oh ee <u>krahm</u>·pee/oo·neen·feh·<u>tsyoh</u>·neh vah·jee·<u>nah</u>·leh*
I missed my period.	**Non ho avuto il ciclo.** *nohn oh ah·<u>voo</u>·toh eel <u>chee</u>·kloh*
I'm on the Pill.	**Prendo la pillola.** *<u>prehn</u>·doh lah <u>peel</u>·loh·lah*
I'm (not) pregnant.	**(Non) Sono incinta.** *(nohn) <u>soh</u>·noh een·<u>cheen</u>·tah*
My last period was…	**Ho avuto l'ultimo ciclo…** *oh ah·<u>voo</u>·toh <u>lool</u>·tee·moh <u>chee</u>·kloh…*

Optician

I've lost…	**Ho perso…** *oh <u>pehr</u>·soh…*
a contact lens	**una lente a contatto** *<u>oo</u>·nah <u>lehn</u>teh ah kohn·<u>tahtt</u>oh*
my glasses	**gli occhiali** *lyee ohk·<u>kyah</u>·lee*
a lens	**una lente** *<u>oo</u>·nah <u>lehn</u>·teh*

Payment & Insurance

How much?	**Quanto costa?** *<u>kwahn</u>·toh <u>koh</u>·stah*
Can I pay by credit card?	**Posso pagare con carta di credito?** *<u>poh</u>·soh pah·<u>gah</u>·reh kohn <u>kahr</u>·tah dee <u>kreh</u>·dee·toh*
I have insurance.	**Ho l'assicurazione.** *oh lahs·see·koo·rah·<u>tsyoh</u>·neh*
I need a receipt for my insurance.	**Mi serve una ricevuta per l'assicurazione.** *mee <u>sehr</u>·veh <u>oo</u>·nah ree·cheh·<u>voo</u>·tah pehr lahs·see·koo·rah·<u>tsyoh</u>·neh*

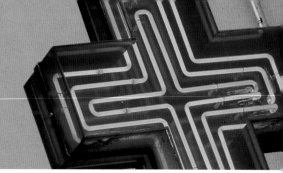

Pharmacy

ESSENTIAL

Where's the pharmacy?	**Dov'è una farmacia?** doh·_veh_ _oo_·nah fahr·mah·_chee_·ah
What time does it open/close?	**A che ora apre/chiude?** ah keh _oh_·rah _ah_·preh/_kyoo_·deh
What would you recommend for…?	**Cosa consiglierebbe per…?** _koh_·zah kohn·see·llyeh·_rehb_·beh pehr…
How much do I take?	**Quanto ne prendo?** _kwahn_·toh neh _prehn_·doh
Can you fill [make up] this prescription?	**Può darmi questo farmaco?** pwoh _dahr_·mee _kweh_·stoh _fahr_·mah·koh
I'm allergic to…	**Sono allergico m /allergica f a…** _soh_·noh ahl·_lehr_·jee·koh/ahl·_lehr_·jee·kah ah…

What to Take

How much do I take?	**Quanto ne prendo?**	_kwahn_·toh neh _prehn_·doh
How often?	**Con che frequenza?**	kohn keh freh·_kwehn_·tsah
Is it safe for children?	**È per bambini?**	eh pehr bahm·_bee_·nee
I'm taking…	**Prendo…**	_prehn_·doh…
Are there side effects?	**Ha effetti collaterali?**	ah ehf·_feht_·tee kohl·_lah_·teh·_rah_·lee
I need something for…	**Ho bisogno di qualcosa per…**	oh bee·_soh_·nyoh dee kwahl·_koh_·zah pehr…

a cold	**il raffreddore**	eel _rahf_·frehd·_doh_·reh
a cough	**la tosse**	lah _tohs_·seh
diarrhea	**la diarrea**	lah dee·ahr·_reh_·ah
a headache	**il mal di testa**	eel mahl dee tehs·tah
insect bites	**una puntura d'insetto**	_oo_·nah poon·_too_·rah deen·_seht_·toh
car/sea/air motion [travel] sickness	**il mal d'auto/di mare/d'aria**	eel mahl _dow_·toh/dee _mah_·reh/_dah_·ryah
a sore throat	**il mal di gola**	eel mahl dee _goh_·lah
sunburn	**una scottatura**	_oo_·nah _skoht_·tah·_too_·rah
toothache	**Il mal di denti**	Eel mahl dee dehn·tee
an upset stomach	**lo stomaco in disordine**	loh _stoh_·mah·koh een dee·_zohr_·dee·neh

Pharmacies are usually open from 8:30 a.m. 12:30 p.m. and 3:30 p.m. 7:30 p.m. In larger cities there is often a **farmacia di turno** available; this pharmacy will have extended hours during the week, weekend and on holidays.
In an emergency, dial 118 for an ambulance.

YOU MAY SEE…

UNA/TRE VOLTE AL GIORNO	once/three times a day
COMPRESSA	tablet
GOCCIA	drop
CUCCHIAINO	teaspoon
DOPO I/PRIMA DEI/CON I PASTI	after/before/with meals
A STOMACO VUOTO	on an empty stomach
DA INGHIOTTIRE INTERA	swallow whole
PUÒ PROVOCARE SONNOLENZA	may cause drowsiness
SOLO PER USO ESTERNO	for external use only

Basic Supplies

I'd like… **Vorrei…** vohr•_ray_…

acetaminophen **del paracetamolo** dehl pah•rah•cheh•tah•_moh_•loh
[paracetamol]

antiseptic cream **una crema antisettica** _oo_•nah _kreh_•mah
ahn•tee•_seht_•tee•kah

aspirin **dell'aspirina** dehl•_lah_•spee•_ree_•nah

bandages **delle fasce** _dehl_•leh _fah_•sheh

a comb **un pettine** oon _peht_•tee•neh

condoms **dei preservativi** day preh•sehr•vah•_tee_•vee

contact lens **una soluzione per le lenti a contatto**
solution _oo_•nah soh•loo•_tsyoh_•neh pehr leh _lehn_•tee
ah kohn•_taht_•toh

deodorant **un deodorante** oon deh•oh•doh•_rahn_•teh

a hairbrush **una spazzola** _oo_•nah _spah_•tsoh•lah

hairspray **una lacca** _oo_•nah _lahk_•kah

ibuprofen **dell'ibuprofene** dehl•lee•boo•proh•_feh_•neh

insect repellent	**un repellente per gli insetti** *oon reh·pehl·lehn·teh pehr llyeen·seht·tee*
lotion	**una lozione** *oo·nah loh·tsyoh·neh*
a nail file	**una limetta per le unghie** *oo·nah lee·meht·tah pehr leh oon·ghyeh*
soap	**una saponetta** *oo·nah sah·poh·neht·tah*
a (disposable) razor	**una lametta (usa e getta)** *oo·nah lah·meht·tah (oo·zah eh jeht·tah)*
razor blades	**delle lamette per rasoio** *dehl·leh lah·meht·teh pehr rah·zoh·yoh*
sanitary napkins [towels]	**un pacco di assorbenti** *oon pahk·koh dee ahs·sohr·behn·tee*
shampoo/ conditioner	**uno shampoo/un balsamo** *oo·noh shahm·pooh/oon bahl·sah·moh*
sunscreen	**un filtro solare** *oon feel·troh soh·lah·reh*
tampons	**una scatola di tamponi** *oo·nah ska·toh·lah dee tahm·poh·nee*
tissues	**dei fazzoletti di carta** *day fah·tsoh·leht·tee dee kahr·tah*
toilet paper	**della carta igienica** *dehl·lah kahr·tah ee·jyeh·nee·kah*
toothpaste	**un dentifricio** *oon dehn·tee·free·chyoh*

For Baby Essentials, see page 145.

The Basics

Grammar

In Italian, there are four forms for 'you' (taking different verb forms): **tu** (singular) and **voi** (plural) are used informally, when talking to relatives, close friends and children (and among young people); the polite form **Lei** (singular) and **loro** (plural) are used in all other cases. If in doubt, use **Lei/loro**. The following abbreviations are used in this section: sing. = singular; pl. = plural; inf. = informal; for. = formal.

Regular Verbs

There are three verb types: infinitives ending in **-are**, **-ere** and **-ire**, e.g. **parlare** (to speak), **vendere** (to sell) and **dormire** (to sleep). Following are sample conjugations for each verb type.

PARLARE (to speak, to talk)		Present	Past	Future
I	**io**	parl**o**	ho parlato	parl**erò**
you (sing.) (inf.)	**tu**	parl**i**	hai parlato	parl**erai**
he/she/you (sing.) (for.)	**lui/lei/Lei**	parl**a**	ha parlato	parl**erà**
we	**noi**	parl**iamo**	abbiamo parlato	parl**eremo**
you (pl.) (inf.)	**voi**	parl**ate**	avete parlato	parl**erete**
they/you (pl.) (for.)	**loro**	parl**ano**	hanno parlato	parl**eranno**

VENDERE (to sell)		Present	Past	Future
I	**io**	vend**o**	ho venduto	vend**erò**
you (sing.) (inf.)	**tu**	vend**i**	hai venduto	vend**erai**
he/she/you (sing.) (for.)	**lui/lei/Lei**	vend**e**	ha venduto	vend**erà**

we	noi	vendiamo	abbiamo venduto	venderemo
you (pl.) (inf.)	voi	vendete	avete venduto	venderete
they/you (pl.) (for.)	loro	vendono	hanno venduto	venderanno

DORMIRE (to sleep)		Present	Past	Future
I	io	dormo	ho dormito	dormirò
you (sing.) (inf.)	tu	dormi	hai dormito	dormirai
he/she/you (sing.) (for.)	lui/lei/Lei	dorme	ha dormito	dormirà
we	noi	dormiamo	abbiamo dormito	dormiremo
you (pl.) (inf.)	voi	dormite	avete dormito	dormirete
they/you (pl.) (for.)	loro	dormono	hanno dormito	dormiranno

Irregular Verbs

There are many irregular verbs whose forms do not follow the regular patterns. The following are the present, past and future forms of **essere** (to be) and **avere** (to have).

ESSERE (to be)		Present	Past	Future
I	io	sono	sono stato	sarò
you (sing.) (inf.)	tu	sei	sei stato	sarai
he/she/you (sing.) (for)	lui/lei/Lei	è	è stato	sarà
we	noi	siamo	siamo stati	saremo
you (pl.) (inf.)	voi	siete	siete stati	sarete
they/you (pl.) (for.)	loro	sono	sono stati	saranno

163

AVERE (to have)			Present	Past	Future
I	**io**	ho	ho avuto	avrò	
you (sing.) (inf.)	**tu**	hai	hai avuto	avrai	
he/she/you (sing.) (for.)	**lui/lei/Lei**	ha	ha avuto	avrà	
we	**noi**	abbiamo	abbiamo avuto	avremo	
you (pl.) (inf.)	**voi**	avete	avete avuto	avrete	
they/you (pl.) (for.)	**loro**	hanno	hanno avuto	avranno	

Word Order

Italian sentences generally follow the subject-verb-object pattern, as in English.

Example: **Vorrei un taxi subito.** I'd like a taxi now.

In Italian, adjectives usually follow the noun.

Example: **un'auto economica** a cheap car (literally, a car cheap)

To form a question in Italian, you can raise the intonation at the end of the sentence, as in English, or use a question word.

Examples:

Lei parla italiano./Lei parla italiano?

You speak Italian./Do you speak Italian?

Quanto costa?

How much?

Negations

To form the negative, use **non** before the conjugated verb.

Example: **Parlo inglese./Non parlo inglese.**

I speak English./I don't speak English.

Imperatives

The imperative, or command form, of Italian verbs is used to give orders or advice. Signs are often in the imperative form. It is formed by adding a specific ending to the stem of the verb (add **–i** to **–are** verbs, and **–a** to **–ere** and **–**

ire verbs). To say the negative, add **non** before the verb. The following are the polite ways to say common commands in Italian:

Fermi!	**Avanti!**	**Non parli!**
Stop!	Go!	Don't speak!

To say 'Let's...' add **–iamo** to the stem of the verb.

Andiamo!	**Finiamo!**
Let's go!	Let's finish!

Nouns & Articles

Generally nouns ending in **–o** are masculine, their plural ending changing to **–i**. Those ending in **–a** are usually feminine, their plural ending changing to **–e**. Nouns ending in **–e** can be either gender changing to **–i** in the plural. The definite articles (the) are **il** *m* and **la** *f*; **l'** is used for singular masculine or feminine nouns that begin with a vowel. The plural forms are **l** *m* and **le** *f*. When a masculine noun begins with **z** or **s** + consonant, the singular article changes to **lo**, the plural to **gli**. **Gli** is also used before plural masculine nouns that begin with a vowel.

The indefinite articles (a, an) also indicate gender: a masculine noun uses **un**, or **uno** when the noun begins with **z** or **s** + consonant. The feminine noun takes **una**, or **un'** when the noun begins with a vowel.

When prepositions are followed by definite articles, they sometimes combine to form one word. For example: **di + el = del**; **di + lo = dello**; **di + l' = dell'**; **di + i = dei**; **di + gli = degli**; **di + la = della**; **di + le = delle**.

Adjectives

Adjectives modify nouns and must agree with the noun in both gender and number. Adjectives ending in **–o** can have four forms, matching the noun:

Masculine, singular: end in **–o: ragazzo italiano** (Italian boy)

Masculine, plural: end in **–i: ragazzi italiani** (Italian boys)

Feminine, singular: end in **–a: signora italiana** (Italian woman)

Feminine, plural: end in **–e: signore italiane** (Italian women)

Adjectives ending in **−e** are the same for masculine and feminine singular, and change to **−i** in the masculine and feminine plural forms.

Example: **ragazzo inglese** (English boy); **ragazza inglese** (English girl); **ragazzi inglesi** (English boys); **ragazze inglesi** (English girls)

Comparatives & Superlatives

To say 'more', use **più**. To say 'less' use **meno**. To say 'the most' or 'the least, use **più** or **meno**, respectively, preceded by the definite article.

Examples:

casa grande/casa più grande/la casa più grande
large house/larger house/the largest house

borsa piccola/borsa più piccola/la borsa più piccola
small bag/smaller bag/the smallest bag

Possessive Pronouns & Adjectives

The following are the Italian forms of possessive pronouns/adjectives. Note that the gender and number agree with the noun, not the speaker.

	masculine, singular	masculine, plural	feminine, singular	feminine, plural
my, mine	**il mio**	**i miei**	**la mia**	**le mie**
your, yours	**il tuo**	**i tuoi**	**la tua**	**le tue**
his, her, hers, its, yours (sing.) (for.)	**il suo**	**i suoi**	**la sua**	**le sue**
our, ours	**il nostro**	**i nostri**	**la nostra**	**le nostre**
your, yours	**il vostro**	**i vostri**	**la vostra**	**le vostre**
their, theirs, yours (pl.) (for.)	**il loro**	**i loro**	**la loro**	**le loro**

Adverbs & Adverbial Expressions

Some Italian adverbs are formed by adding **–mente** to the feminine singular form of the adjective.

Example: **lento** *m* /**lenta** *f* (slow), **lentamente** (slowly)

If the adjective ends in **–le** or **–re**, drop the **–e** and add **–mente**.

Example: **facile** (easy), **facilmente** (easily)

Numbers

ESSENTIAL

0	**zero** *dzeh·roh*	
1	**uno** *oo·noh*	
2	**due** *doo·eh*	
3	**tre** *treh*	
4	**quattro** *kwaht·troh*	
5	**cinque** *cheen·kweh*	
6	**sei** *say*	
7	**sette** *seht·teh*	
8	**otto** *oht·toh*	
9	**nove** *noh·veh*	
10	**dieci** *dyeh·chee*	
11	**undici** *oon·dee·chee*	
12	**dodici** *doh·dee·chee*	
13	**tredici** *treh·dee·chee*	
14	**quattordici** *kwaht·tohr·dee·chee*	
15	**quindici** *kween·dee·chee*	
16	**sedici** *seh·dee·chee*	
17	**diciassette** *dee·chyahs·seht·teh*	
18	**diciotto** *dee·chyoht·toh*	
19	**diciannove** *dee·chyahn·noh·veh*	

20	**venti** _vehn_·tee
21	**ventuno** vehn·_too_·noh
22	**ventidue** vehn·tee·_doo_·eh
30	**trenta** _trehn_·tah
31	**trentuno** trehn·_too_·noh
40	**quaranta** kwah·_rahn_·tah
50	**cinquanta** cheen·_kwahn_·tah
60	**sessanta** sehs·_sahn_·tah
70	**settanta** seht·_tahn_·tah
80	**ottanta** oht·_tahn_·tah
90	**novanta** noh·_vahn_·tah
100	**cento** _chehn_·toh
101	**centuno** chehn·_too_·noh
200	**duecento** doo·eh·_chehn_·toh
500	**cinquecento** cheen·kweh·_chehn_·toh
1,000	**mille** _meel_·leh
10,000	**diecimila** dyeh·chee·_mee_·lah
1,000,000	**milione** mee·_lyoh_·neh

Ordinal Numbers

first	**primo** _pree_·moh
second	**secondo** seh·_kohn_·doh
third	**terzo** _tehr_·tsoh
fourth	**quarto** _kwahr_·toh
fifth	**quinto** _kween_·toh
once	**una volta** _oo_·nah _vohl_·tah
twice	**due volte** _doo_·eh _vohl_·teh
three times	**tre volte** treh _vohl_·teh

Time

ESSENTIAL

What time is it?	**Che ore sono?**	keh <u>oh</u>·reh <u>soh</u>·noh
It's noon [midday].	**È mezzogiorno.**	eh meh·dzoh·<u>jyohr</u>·noh
At midnight.	**A mezzanotte.**	ah meh·dzah·<u>noht</u>·teh
From one o'clock to two o'clock.	**Dall'una alle due.**	dahl·<u>loo</u>·nah <u>ahl</u>·leh <u>doo</u>·eh
Five after [past] three.	**Le tre e cinque.**	leh treh eh <u>cheen</u>·kweh
A quarter to three.	**Sono le tre meno un quarto.**	<u>soh</u>·noh leh treh <u>meh</u>·noh oon <u>kwahr</u>·toh
5:30 a.m./5:30 p.m.	**le cinque e mezzo/le diciassette e trenta**	leh <u>cheen</u>·kweh eh <u>meh</u>·dzoh/ leh <u>dee</u>·chyahs·<u>seht</u>·teh eh <u>trehn</u>·tah

Days

ESSENTIAL

Monday	**lunedì**	loon·eh·<u>dee</u>
Tuesday	**martedì**	mahr·teh·<u>dee</u>
Wednesday	**mercoledì**	mehr·koh·leh·<u>dee</u>
Thursday	**giovedì**	jyoh·veh·<u>dee</u>
Friday	**venerdì**	veh·nehr·<u>dee</u>
Saturday	**sabato**	<u>sah</u>·bah·toh
Sunday	**domenica**	doh·<u>meh</u>·nee·kah

Dates

yesterday	**ieri** _yeh_·ree
today	**oggi** _oh_·djee
tomorrow	**domani** doh·_mah_·nee
day	**giorno** _jyohr_·noh
week	**settimana** seht·tee·_mah_·nah
month	**mese** _meh_·zeh
year	**anno** _ahn_·noh

Months

January	**gennaio** jehn·_nah_·yoh
February	**febbraio** fehb·_brah_·yoh
March	**marzo** _mahr_·tsoh
April	**aprile** ah·_pree_·leh
May	**maggio** _mah_·djoh
June	**giugno** _jyoo_·nyoh
July	**luglio** _loo_·llyoh
August	**agosto** ah·_goh_·stoh
September	**settembre** seht·_tehm_·breh
October	**ottobre** oht·_toh_·breh
November	**novembre** noh·_vehm_·breh
December	**dicembre** dee·_chem_·breh

Lunedì (Monday) is the first day of the week; **domenica** (Sunday) is the last. Italian does not capitalize the names of days.

Italy follows a day-month-year format instead of the month-day-year format used in the U.S.
For example, July 25, 2008; 25/07/08 = 7/25/2008 in the U.S.

Seasons

in/during...	**in/durante...** *een/doo-<u>rahn</u>-teh...*
the spring	**la primavera** *lah pree-mah-<u>veh</u>-rah*
the summer	**l'estate** *leh-<u>stah</u>-teh*
the fall [autumn]	**l'autunno** *l-ow-<u>toon</u>-noh*
the winter	**l'inverno** *leen-<u>vehr</u>-noh*

Holidays

January 1: **Capodanno** New Year's Day
January 6: **Epifania** Epiphany
April 25: **Festa della Liberazione** Liberation Day
May 1: **Festa dei Lavoratori** Labor Day
August 15: **Ferragosto** Assumption Day
November 1: **Ognissanti** All Saints Day
December 8: **Immacolata Concezione** Immaculate Conception
December 25: **Natale** Christmas Day
December 26: **Santo Stefano** St. Stephen's Day
Moveable dates include:
Venerdì Santo Good Friday
Pasqua Easter Day
Pasquetta Easter Monday

Conversion Tables

When you know	Multiply by	To find
ounces	28.3	grams
pounds	0.45	kilograms
inches	2.54	centimeters
feet	0.3	meters
miles	1.61	kilometers
square inches	6.45	sq. centimeters
square feet	0.09	sq. meters
square miles	2.59	sq. kilometers
pints (U.S./Brit.)	0.47/0.56	liters
gallons (U.S./Brit.)	3.8/4.5	liters
Fahrenheit	5/9, after 32	Centigrade
Centigrade	9/5, then +32	Fahrenheit

Kilometers to Miles Conversions

1 km – 0.62 mi	20 km – 12.4 mi
5 km – 3.10 mi	50 km – 31.0 mi
10 km – 6.20 mi	100 km – 61.0 mi

Measurement

1 gram (gr)	**1 grammo**	= 0.035 oz.
1/10 of a kilo	**etto** (sing.)/**etti** (pl.)	= 0.22 lb
1 kilogram (kg)	**1 chilo**	= 2.2 lb
1 liter (l)	**1 litro**	= 1.06 U.S./ 0.88 Brit. quarts
1 centimeter (cm)	**1 centimetro**	= 0.4 inch
1 meter (m)	**1 metro**	= 3.28 ft.
1 kilometer (km)	**1 chilometro**	= 0.62 mile

Temperature

-40° C – -40° F	-1° C – 30° F	20° C – 68° F
-30° C – -22° F	0° C – 32° F	25° C – 77° F
-20° C – -4° F	5° C – 41° F	30° C – 86° F
-10° C – 14° F	10° C – 50° F	35° C – 95° F
-5° C – 23° F	15° C – 59° F	

Oven Temperature

100° C – 212° F	177° C – 350° F
121° C – 250° F	204° C – 400° F
149° C – 300° F	260° C – 500° F

Dictionary

A

a.m. del mattino
abbey l'abbazia
accept v accettare
access l'accesso
accident l'incidente
accommodation l'alloggio
account il conto
acupuncture l'agopuntura
adapter l'adattatore
address l'indirizzo
admission l'ingresso
after dopo; **~noon** il pomeriggio;
  ~shave il dopobarba
age l'età
agency l'agenzia
AIDS l'AIDS
air l'aria; **~ conditioning** l'aria
  condizionata; **~ pump** la
  pompa dell'aria; **~line** la
  compagnia aerea; **~mail** la
  posta aerea; **~plane** l'aereo;
  ~port l'aeroporto
aisle il corridoio; **~ seat** il posto
  sul corridoio

allergic allergico; **~ reaction**
  la reazione allergica
allow v permettere
alone solo
alter v modificare
alternate route il percorso
  alternativo
aluminum foil la carta stagnola
amazing straordinario
ambulance l'ambulanza
American americano
amusement park il lunapark
anemic anemico
anesthesia l'anestesia
animal l'animale
ankle la caviglia
antibiotic l'antibiotico
antiques store il negozio
  d'antiquariato
antiseptic cream la crema
  antisettica
anything qualsiasi cosa
apartment l'appartamento
appendix (body part) l'appendice
appetizer l'antipasto

adj adjective	**BE** British English	**v** verb
adv adverb	**n** noun	

appointment l'appuntamento
arcade la sala giochi
area code il prefisso
arm il braccio
aromatherapy l'aromaterapia
around (the corner) dietro di
arrivals (airport) gli arrivi
arrive v arrivare
artery l'arteria
arthritis l'artrite
art l'arte
aspirin l'aspirina
asthmatic asmatico
ATM il bancomat
attack l'aggressione
attend v frequentare
attraction (place) l'attrattiva
attractive attraente
Australia Australia
Australian australiano
automatic automatico; **~ car**
l'auto col cambio automatico
available libero

B

baby il bebè; **~ bottle** il biberon;
~ wipe la salvietta per neonati;
~sitter la babysitter
back (body part) la schiena;
~ache il mal di schiena;
~pack lo zaino

bag la borsa
baggage il bagaglio; **~ claim** il
ritiro bagagli; **~ ticket** lo
scontrino bagagli
bakery la panetteria
ballet lo spettacolo di danza
bandage la benda
bank la banca
bar il bar
barbecue il barbecue
barber il barbiere
baseball il baseball
basket (grocery store) il cestino
basketball il basketball
bathroom il bagno
battery la batteria
battleground il campo di battaglia
be v essere
beach la spiaggia
beautiful bello
bed il letto; **~ and breakfast**
la pensione
begin v iniziare
before prima
beginner il principiante
behind dietro
beige beige
belt la cintura
berth la cuccetta
best il migliore
better migliore

bicycle la bicicletta

big grande

bigger più grande

bike route il percorso ciclabile

bikini il bikini; ~ **wax** la ceretta
   all'inguine

bill v **(charge)** fatturare;
   ~ n **(money)** la banconota;
   ~ n **(of sale)** il conto

bird l'uccello

birthday il compleanno

black nero

bladder la vescica

bland insipido

blanket la coperta

bleed v sanguinare

blood il sangue; ~ **pressure** la
   pressione sanguigna

blouse la camicetta

blue blu

board v imbarcarsi

boarding pass la carta d'imbarco

boat la barca

bone l'osso

book il libro; ~**store** la libreria

boots gli stivali

boring noioso

botanical garden il giardino
   botanico

bother v infastidire

bottle la bottiglia;

~ **opener** l'apribottiglie

bowl la coppa

box la scatola

boxing match l'incontro di boxe

boy il ragazzo; ~**friend** il ragazzo

bra il reggiseno

bracelet il braccialetto

brakes (car) i freni

break v rompere; ~**-in**
   (burglary) il furto con scasso;
   ~**down** il guasto

breakfast la colazione

breast il petto; ~**feed** v allattare

breathe v respirare

bridge il ponte

briefs (clothing) lo slip

bring v portare

British inglese

broken rotto

brooch la spilla

broom la scopa

brother il fratello

brown marrone

bug l'insetto

building l'edificio

burn v bruciare

bus l'autobus; ~ **station**
   la stazione degli autobus;
   ~ **stop** la fermata del bus;
   ~ **ticket** il biglietto del bus;
   ~ **tour** l'escursione in pullman

business il lavoro; ~ **card** il biglietto da visita; ~ **center** il centro business; ~ **class** la classe business; ~ **hours** l'orario d'apertura

butcher il macellaio

buttocks le natiche

buy *v* comprare

bye ciao

C

cabaret il cabaret

cabin la cabina

cable car la funivia

cafe il caffè

call *v* chiamare; ~ *n* la chiamata

calories le calorie

camera la macchina fotografica; **digital** ~ la macchina fotografica digitale; ~ **case** l'astuccio della macchina fotografica; ~ **store** il negozio di fotografia

camp *v* campeggiare; ~ **stove** il fornello da campeggio; ~**site** il campeggio

can opener l'apriscatole

Canada il Canada

Canadian canadese

cancel *v* annullare

candy le caramelle

canned good lo scatolame

canyon il canalone

car l'auto; ~ **hire [BE]** l'autonoleggio; ~ **park [BE]** il parcheggio; ~ **rental** l'autonoleggio; ~ **seat** il seggiolino per auto

carafe la caraffa

card la carta; **ATM** ~ il bancomat; **credit** ~ la carta di credito; **debit** ~ il bancomat; **phone** ~ la scheda telefonica

carry on board *v* **[BE]** portare a bordo

carry-on il bagaglio a mano

cart (grocery store) il carrello; ~ **(luggage)** il carrello

carton il cartone; ~ **of cigarettes** la stecca di sigarette

case (container) la cassa

cash *v* incassare; ~ *n* i contanti; ~ **advance** l'acconto

cashier il cassiere

casino il casinò

castle il castello

cathedral la cattedrale

cave la grotta

CD il CD

cell phone il telefonino

Celsius Celsius

centimeter il centimetro

certificate il certificato

chair la sedia; **~ lift** la seggiovia

change *v* **(buses)** cambiare;
~ *v* **(money)** cambiare;
~ *v* **(baby)** cambiare;
~ *n* **(money)** il cambio

charcoal il carbone

charge *v* **(credit card)** addebitare;
~ *n* **(cost)** il costo

cheap economico; **~er** più
economico

check *v* **(on something)**
controllare; **~** *v* **(luggage)**
controllare; **~** *n* **(payment)**
l'assegno; **~-in (hotel/airport)**
il check-in; **~ing account**
il conto corrente; **~-out (hotel)**
il pagamento del conto

Cheers! Salute!

chemical toilet il WC da
campeggio

chemist [BE] la farmacia

cheque [BE] l'assegno

chest (body part) il petto;
~ pain il dolore al petto

chewing gum la gomma da
masticare

child il bambino; **~ seat** il
seggiolone; **~'s menu** il menù per
bambino; **~'s portion** la porzione
per bambino

Chinese cinese

chopsticks i bastoncini cinesi

church la chiesa

cigar il sigaro

cigarette la sigaretta

class la classe; **business ~**
la classe business; **economy ~**
la classe economica; **first ~**
la prima classe

classical music la musica classica

clean *v* pulire; **~** *adj* pulito; **~ing
product** il prodotto per la pulizia;
~ing supplies i prodotti per la
pulizia

clear *v* **(on an ATM)** cancellare

cliff la scogliera

cling film [BE] la pellicola per
alimenti

close *v* **(a shop)** chiudere

close vicino

closed chiuso

clothing l'abbigliamento;
~ store il negozio
d'abbigliamento

club il club

coat il cappotto

coffee shop il caffè

coin la moneta

colander la scolapasta

cold (sickness) il raffreddore;
~ (temperature) freddo

colleague il collega

cologne la colonia
color il colore
comb il pettine
come v venire
complaint il reclamo
computer il computer
concert il concerto; ~ **hall** la sala
  da concerti
condition (medical) la condizione
conditioner il balsamo
condom il preservativo
conference la conferenza
confirm v confermare
congestion la congestione
connect v **(internet)** collegarsi
connection (internet)
  il collegamento; ~ **(flight)**
  la coincidenza
constipated costipato
consulate il consolato
consultant il consulente
contact v contattare; ~ **lens** la
  lente a contatto; ~ **lens**
  solution la soluzione per lenti a
  contatto
contagious contagioso
convention hall la sala congressi
conveyor belt il nastro
  trasportatore
cook v cucinare
cooking gas il gas per cucina

cool (temperature) fresco
copper il rame
corkscrew il cavatappi
cost v costare
cot il lettino
cotton il cotone
cough v tossire; ~ n la tosse
country code il prefisso del paese
cover charge il coperto
crash v **(car)** fare un incidente
cream (ointment) la crema
credit card la carta di credito
crew neck a girocollo
crib la culla
crystal il cristallo
cup la tazza
currency la valuta; ~ **exchange**
  il cambio valuta; ~ **exchange**
  office l'ufficio di cambio
current account [BE] il conto
  corrente
customs la dogana
cut v (hair) tagliare;
  ~ n **(injury)** il taglio
cute carino
cycling il ciclismo

D

damage v danneggiare;
  ~**d** danneggiato
dance v ballare; ~ **club** il club di

ballo; ~**ing** il ballo
dangerous pericoloso
dark scuro
date (calendar) la data
day il giorno
deaf sordo
debit card il bancomat
deck chair la sedia a sdraio
declare v dichiarare
decline v **(credit card)** rifiutare
deeply profondamente
degrees (temperature) i gradi
delay v ritardare
delete v **(computer)** eliminare
delicatessen la gastronomia
delicious squisito
denim i jeans
dentist il dentista
denture la dentiera
deodorant il deodorante
department store il grande
  magazzino
departures (airport) le partenze
deposit v depositare;
  ~ **(bank)** n il deposito;
  ~ **(to reserve a room)** il deposito
desert il deserto
detergent il detersivo
develop v **(film)** sviluppare
diabetic diabetico
dial v comporre il numero

diamond il diamante
diaper il pannolino
diarrhea la diarrea
diesel il diesel
difficult difficile
digital digitale; ~ **camera** la
  macchina fotografica digitale;
  ~ **photos** le foto digitali;
  ~ **prints** le stampe digitali
dining room la sala da pranzo
dinner la cena
direction la direzione
dirty sporco
disabled il disabile; ~ **accessible**
  [BE] accessibile ai disabili
disconnect v (computer) scollegare
discount lo sconto
dish (kitchen) il piatto;
  ~**washer** la lavastoviglie;
  ~**washing liquid** il detersivo per
  i piatti
display lo schermo; ~ **case** la
  vetrinetta
disposable usa e getta; ~ **razor**
  la lametta usa e getta
dive v tuffarsi; ~**ing**
  equipment l'attrezzatura
  subacquea
divorce v divorziare
dizzy stordito
doctor il medico

doll la bambola

dollar (U.S.) il dollaro

domestic domestico; ~ **flight** il volo nazionale

door la porta

dormitory il dormitorio

double bed il letto matrimoniale

downtown (direction) il centro; ~ **area** il centro

dozen la dozzina

drag lift lo ski lift

dress (piece of clothing) il vestito; ~ **code** il codice di abbigliamento

drink v bere; ~ n la bevanda; ~ **menu** il menù delle bevande; ~**ing water** l'acqua potabile

drive v guidare

driver's license number il numero di patente

drop (medicine) la goccia

drowsiness la sonnolenza

dry cleaner il lavasecco

dubbed doppiato

during durante

duty (tax) la tassa; ~ **free** duty free

DVD il DVD

E

ear l'orecchio; ~**ache** il mal d'orecchio

earlier prima

early presto

earrings gli orecchini

east est

easy facile

eat v mangiare

economy class la classe economica

elbow il gomito

electric outlet la presa elettrica

elevator l'ascensore

e-mail v inviare e-mail; ~ n l'e-mail; ~ **address** l'indirizzo e-mail

emergency l'emergenza; ~ **exit** l'uscita d'emergenza

empty v svuotare

enamel (jewelry) lo smalto

end v finire

English inglese

engrave v incidere

enjoy v godersi

enter v entrare

entertainment l'intrattenimento

entrance l'entrata

envelope la busta

equipment l'attrezzatura

escalators le scale mobili

estate car [BE] la station wagon

e-ticket il biglietto elettronico

EU resident il residente UE

euro l'euro

evening la sera
excess l'eccesso
exchange v (money) cambiare;
  ~ **n (place)** il cambio;
  ~ **rate** il tasso di cambio
excursion l'escursione
excuse v scusare
exhausted esausto
exit v uscire; ~ n l'uscita
expensive caro
expert esperto
exposure (film) la posa
express espresso; ~ **bus** il bus
  espresso; ~ **train** il treno espresso
extension (phone) l'interno
extra extra; ~ **large** extra large
extract v **(tooth)** estrarre
eye l'occhio
eyebrow wax la ceretta per
  sopracciglie

F

face il viso
facial la pulizia del viso
family la famiglia
fan (appliance) il ventilatore;
  ~ **(souvenir)** il ventaglio
far lontano; ~**-sighted**
  ipermetrope
farm la fattoria
fast veloce; ~ **food** il fast food

faster più veloce
fat free senza grassi
father il padre
fax v inviare per fax; ~ n il fax;
  ~ **number** il numero di fax
fee la tariffa
feed v dare da mangiare
ferry il traghetto
fever la febbre
field (sports) il campo
fill v riempire; ~ **out** v
  (form) compilare; ~**ing**
  (tooth) l'otturazione
film (camera) il rullino
fine (fee for breaking law)
  la multa
finger il dito; ~**nail** l'unghia
fire il fuoco; ~ **department** i vigili
  del fuoco; ~ **door** la porta
  antincendio
first primo; ~ **class** la prima classe
fit (clothing) v andare bene
fitting room il camerino
fix v **(repair)** riparare
flashlight la torcia elettrica
flat tire la gomma a terra
flight il volo
floor il pavimento
flower il fiore
folk music la musica folk
food il cibo

foot il piede
football game [BE] la partita di football
for per
forecast la previsione
forest il bosco
fork la forchetta
form il modulo
formula (baby) il latte in polvere
fort la fortezza
fountain la fontana
free libero
freezer il freezer
fresh fresco
friend l'amico
frying pan la padella
full-service il servizio completo
full-time a tempo pieno

G

game la partita
garage il garage
garbage bag il sacchetto per la spazzatura
gas (cooking) il gas per cucina; ~ **(heating)** il gas; ~ **station** la stazione del servizio; ~ **(vehicle)** la benzina
gate (airport) l'uscita
gay gay; ~ **bar** il bar per gay; ~ **club** il club per gay

gel (hair) il gel
get off v **(a train/bus/subway)** scendere
get to v arrivare
gift il regalo; ~ **shop** il negozio di articoli da regalo
girl la ragazza; ~**friend** la ragazza
give v dare
glass (drinking) il bicchiere; ~ **(material)** il vetro; ~**es** gli occhiali
go v **(somewhere)** andare
gold l'oro
golf golf; ~ **course** il campo da golf; ~ **club** la mazza; ~ **tournament** la gara di golf
good n il bene; ~ adj buono; ~ **afternoon** buon pomeriggio; ~ **evening** buonasera; ~ **morning** buongiorno; ~ **bye** arrivederla; ~**s** le merci
gram il grammo
grandchild il nipote
grandparent il nonno
gray grigio
green verde
grocery store il fruttivendolo
ground floor il pianterreno
groundcloth [groundsheet BE] il telone impermeabile
group il gruppo

guide la guida; **~ book** la guida; **~ dog** il cane da guida

gym la palestra

gynecologist il ginecologo

H

hair i capelli; **~ dryer** l'asciugacapelli; **~ salon** il parrucchiere; **~brush** la spazzola ; **~ cut** il taglio; **~spray** la lacca; **~style** l'acconciatura; **~stylist** il parrucchiere

half la metà; **~ hour** la mezz'ora; **~-kilo** il mezzo chilo

hammer il martello

hand la mano; **~ luggage** il bagaglio a mano; **~bag** la borsetta

handicapped il disabile; **~ accessible** accessibile ai disabili

hangover la sbornia

happy felice

hat il cappello

have v avere

head (body part) la testa; **~ache** il mal di testa; **~phones** gli auricolari

health la salute; **~ food store** l'erboristeria

heart il cuore; **~ condition** il disturbo cardiaco

heat il calore; **~er** il radiatore

hello salve

helmet il casco

help v aiutare; **~** n l'aiuto

here qui

heterosexual eterosessuale

hi ciao

high alto; **~chair** il seggiolone; **~-heeled shoes** le scarpe col tacco alto; **~way** l'autostrada

hiking boots gli scarponi da montagna

hill la collina

hire v [BE] noleggiare; **~ car [BE]** l'auto a noleggio

hitchhike v fare l'autostop

hockey l'hockey

holiday [BE] la vacanza

horse track l'ippodromo

hospital l'ospedale

hostel l'ostello

hot (temperature) caldo; **~ (spicy)** piccante; **~ springs** le terme; **~ water** l'acqua calda

hotel l'hotel

hour l'ora

house la casa; **~hold goods** gli articoli casalinghi; **~keeping services** i servizi di pulizia domestica

how come; ~ **much** quanto
hug *v* abbracciare
hungry affamato
hurt il dolore
husband il marito

I

ibuprofen l'ibuprofene
ice il ghiaccio; ~ **hockey** l'hockey su ghiaccio
icy gelato
identification l'identificazione
ill malato
in in
include *v* includere
indoor pool la piscina interna
inexpensive a buon mercato
infected infetto
information (phone) le informazioni; ~ **desk** l'ufficio informazioni
insect insetto; ~ **bite** la puntura d'insetto; ~ **repellent** il repellente per gli insetti
insert *v* inserire
insomnia l'insonnia
instant message il messaggio istantaneo
insulin l'insulina
insurance l'assicurazione; ~ **card** la tessera dell'assicurazione;

~ **company** la compagnia di assicurazione
interesting interessante
intermediate intermedio
international (airport area) internazionale; ~ **flight** il volo internazionale; ~ **student card** la tessera internazionale dello studente
internet l'Internet; ~ **cafe** l'Internet caffè; ~ **service** il servizio Internet; **wireless** ~ il collegamento wireless a Internet
interpreter l'interprete
intersection l'incrocio
intestine l'intestino
introduce *v* presentare
invoice [BE] la fattura
Ireland l'Irlanda
Irish irlandese
iron *v* stirare; ~ *n* **(clothes)** il ferro da stiro
Italian italiano
Italy l'Italia

J

jacket la giacca
jar il vaso
jaw la mascella
jazz il jazz; ~ **club** il club jazz
jeans i jeans

jet ski l'acquascooter
jeweler il gioielliere
jewelry la gioielleria
join *v* unire
joint (body part) la giuntura

K

key la chiave; ~ **card** la chiave elettronica; ~ **ring** il portachiavi
kiddie pool la piscina per bambini
kidney (body part) il rene
kilo il chilo; ~**gram** il chilogrammo; ~**meter** il chilometro
kiss *v* baciare
kitchen la cucina; ~ **foil** la carta stagnola
knee il ginocchio
knife il coltello

L

lace il pizzo
lactose intolerant intollerante al lattosio
lake il lago
large grande
larger più grande
last ultimo
late (time) tardi
later più tardi
launderette [BE] la lavanderia a gettone

laundromat la lavanderia a gettone
laundry la lavanderia; ~ **facility** il locale lavanderia; ~ **service** il servizio di lavanderia
lawyer l'avvocato
leather la pelle
leave *v* partire
left (direction) a sinistra
leg la gamba
lens la lente
less meno
lesson la lezione
letter la lettera
library la biblioteca
life la vita; ~ **jacket** il giubbotto di salvataggio; ~**guard** il bagnino
lift (ride) il passaggio; ~ **[BE]** l'ascensore; ~ **pass** il lift pass
light (overhead) la lampada; ~ *v* **(cigarette)** accendere; ~**bulb** la lampadina; ~**er** l'accendino
like *v* **(someone)** piacere
line (train) la linea
linen il lino
lip il labbro
liquor store l'enoteca
liter il litro
little piccolo
live *v* vivere

liver (body part) il fegato
loafers i mocassini
local locale
lock v chiudere; ~ n la serratura
locker l'armadietto
log off v **(computer)** fare il logoff
log on v **(computer)** fare il logon
long lungo; ~ **sleeves** le
  maniche lunghe; ~-**sighted**
  [BE] ipermetrope
look v guardare
lose v **(something)** perdere
lost perso; ~ **and found** l'ufficio
  oggetti smarriti
lotion la lozione
louder più forte
love v **(someone)** amare; ~ n
  l'amore
low basso; ~**er** più basso
luggage il bagaglio;
  ~ **cart** il carrello bagagli;
  ~ **locker** l'armadietto dei bagagli;
  ~ **ticket** lo scontrino dei bagagli;
  hand ~ **[BE]** il bagaglio a mano
lunch il pranzo
lung il polmone

M

magazine la rivista
magnificent magnifico
mail v spedire; ~ n la posta;

~**box** la cassetta della posta
main principale; ~ **attraction**
  l'attrattiva principale; ~ **course**
  il piatto principale
make up [BE] (a prescription)
  il trucco
mall il centro commerciale
man l'uomo
manager il responsabile
manicure il manicure
manual car l'auto col cambio
  manuale
map la cartina
market il mercato
married sposato
marry v sposare
mass (church service) la messa
massage il massaggio
match n **(wooden**
  stick) il fiammifero; ~ n
  (game) la partita
meal il pasto
measure v **(someone/**
  something) misurare; ~**ing**
  cup la tazza di misurazione; ~**ing**
  spoon il misurino
mechanic il meccanico
medicine la medicina
medium (size) medio
meet v **(someone)** incontrare
meeting (corporate) la riunione;

~ room sala riunioni
membership card la tessera associativa
memorial (place) il monumento
memory card la scheda memoria
mend v riparare
menstrual cramp il crampo mestruale
menu il menù
message il messaggio
meter (parking) il parchimetro
microwave il microonde
midday [BE] mezzogiorno
midnight mezzanotte
mileage il chilometraggio
mini-bar il minibar
minute il minuto
missing (was never there) mancante; scomparso **(was previously there)**
mistake l'errore
mobile mobile; **~ home** la casa prefabbricata; **~ phone [BE]** il telefonino
mobility la mobilità
money il denaro
month il mese
mop lo spazzolone
moped lo scooter
more più
morning il mattino

mosque la moschea
mother la madre
motor il motore; **~ boat** il motoscafo; **~cycle** la motocicletta; **~way [BE]** l'autostrada
mountain la montagna; **~ bike** la mountain bike
mousse (hair) la mousse
mouth la bocca
movie il film; **~ theater** il cinema
mug v scippare
muscle il muscolo
museum il museo
music la musica; **~ store** il negozio di musica

N

nail l'unghia; **~ file** la lima; **~ salon** il salone di bellezza
name il nome
napkin il tovagliolo
nappy [BE] il pannolino
nationality la nazionalità
nature preserve la riserva naturale
(be) nauseous v avere la nausea
near vicino; **~-sighted** miope
neck il collo; **~lace** la collana
need v necessitare
newspaper il giornale
newsstand l'edicola
next prossimo

nice sympatico
night la notte; **~club** il nightclub
no no
non-alcoholic analcolico
non-smoking non fumatori
noon mezzogiorno
north nord
nose il naso
notes [BE] le banconote
nothing niente
notify v avvertire
novice il principiante
now ora
number il numero
nurse l'infermiere

O

office l'ufficio; **~ hours** l'orario
  d'ufficio
off-licence [BE] l'enoteca
oil l'olio
OK OK
old vecchio
on the corner all'angolo
once una volta
one uno; **~-way (ticket)** solo
  andata; **~-way street** il senso unico
only solo
open v aprire; **~** adj aperto
opera l'opera; **~ house** il teatro
  dell'opera

opposite di fronte a
optician l'ottico
orange (color) arancione
orchestra l'orchestra
order v ordinare
outdoor pool la piscina esterna
outside fuori
over sopra; **~ the counter
  (medication)** da banco; **~look
  (scenic place)** il belvedere;
  ~night per la notte
oxygen treatment
  l'ossigeno terapia

P

p.m. del pomeriggio
pacifier il ciuccio
pack v fare le valigie
package il pacchetto
paddling pool [BE] la piscina per
  bambini
pad [BE] l'assorbente
pain il dolore
pajamas il pigiama
palace il palazzo
pants i pantaloni
pantyhose il collant
paper la carta; **~ towel** la carta
  da cucina
paracetamol [BE] il paracetamolo
park v parcheggiare; **~** n il parco;

~ing garage il parcheggio; **~ing lot** il parcheggio

parliament building l'edificio del parlamento

part (for car) il ricambio; **~ time** part-time

pass through *v* passare

passenger il passeggero

passport il passaporto; **~ control** il controllo passaporti

password la password

pastry shop la pasticceria

path il sentiero

pay *v* pagare; **~ phone** il telefono pubblico

peak (of a mountain) la vetta

pearl la perla

pedestrian il pedone

pediatrician il pediatra

pedicure il pedicure

pen la penna

penicillin la penicillina

penis il pene

per per; **~ day** al giorno; **~ hour** all'ora; **~ night** a notte; **~ week** a settimana

perfume il profumo

period (menstrual) il ciclo; **~ (of time)** il periodo

permit *v* permettere

petite piccolo

petrol [BE] la benzina; **~ station [BE]** la stazione di servizio

pewter il peltro

pharmacy la farmacia

phone *v* telefonare; **~** *n* il telefono; **~ call** la telefonata; **~ card** la scheda telefonica; **~ number** il numero di telefono

photo la foto; **~copy** la fotocopia; **~graphy** la fotografia

pick up *v* **(something)** raccogliere

picnic area la zona picnic

piece il pezzo

Pill (birth control) la pillola

pillow il cuscino

personal identification number (PIN) il codice PIN

pink rosa

piste [BE] la pista; **~ map [BE]** la cartina delle piste

pizzeria la pizzeria

place a bet *v* scommettere

plane l'aereo

plastic wrap la pellicola per alimenti

plate il piatto

platform (train) il binario

platinum il platino

play *v* giocare; **~** *n* **(theater)** lo spettacolo; **~ ground** il parco giochi; **~ pen** il box

please per favore
pleasure il piacere
plunger lo sturalavandini
plus size la taglia forte
pocket la tasca
poison il veleno
poles (skiing) le racchette
police la polizia; ~ **report**
  il verbale di polizia; ~ **station**
  il commissariato
pond lo stagno
pool (swimming) la piscina
pop music la musica pop
portion la porzione
post [BE] la posta; ~ **office**
  l'ufficio postale; ~**box [BE]**
  la buca delle lettere; ~**card**
  la cartolina
pot (for cooking) la pentola;
  ~ **(for flowers)** il vaso
pottery la ceramica
pounds (British sterling)
  le sterline
pregnant incinta
prescribe v prescrivere
prescription la ricetta
press v **(clothing)** stirare
price il prezzo
print v stampare
problem il problema
produce la frutta e verdura;

~ **store** il fruttivendolo
prohibit v proibire
pronounce v pronunciare
public pubblico
pull v **(door sign)** tirare
purple viola
purse la borsetta
push v **(door sign)** spingere;
  ~**chair [BE]** il passeggino

Q

quality la qualità
question la domanda
quiet tranquillo

R

racetrack il circuito
racket (sports) la racchetta
railway station [BE] la stazione
  ferroviaria
rain la pioggia; ~**coat**
  l'impermeabile; ~**forest** la foresta
  pluviale; ~**y** piovoso
rap (music) il rap
rape v stuprare; ~ n lo stupro
rash l'irritazione
razor blade la lametta
reach v raggiungere
ready pronto
real vero
receipt la ricevuta

receive v ricevere
reception la reception
recharge v ricaricare
recommend v raccomandare
recommendation la raccomandazione
recycling il reciclaggio
red rosso
refrigerator il frigorifero
region la regione
registered mail la raccomandata
regular normale
relationship la relazione
rent v affittare
rental car l'auto a noleggio
repair v riparare
repeat v ripetere
reservation la prenotazione; ~ **desk** l'ufficio prenotazioni
reserve v prenotare
restaurant il ristorante
restroom la toilette
retired in pensione
return v (something) portare indietro; ~ n [BE] la resa
rib (body part) la costola
right (direction) a destra; ~ **of way** la precedenza
ring l'anello
river il fiume
road map la cartina stradale

rob v rubare; ~**bed** derubato
romantic romantico
room la stanza; ~ **key** la chiave della stanza; ~ **service** il servizio in camera
round-trip l'andata e ritorno
route il percorso
rowboat la barca a remi
rubbish [BE] la spazzatura; ~ **bag [BE]** il sacchetto per la spazzatura
rugby il rugby
ruins le rovine
rush la fretta

S

sad triste
safe (receptacle) la cassaforte; ~ **(protected)** sicuro
sales tax l'IVA
same stesso
sandals i sandali
sanitary napkin l'assorbente
saucepan la pentola
sauna la sauna
save v (computer) salvare
savings (account) i risparmi
scanner lo scanner
scarf la sciarpa
schedule v programmare; ~ n il programma

school la scuola
science la scienza
scissors le forbici
sea il mare
seat il posto
security la sicurezza
see v vedere
self-service il self-service
sell v vendere
seminar il seminario
send v inviare
senior citizen l'anziano
separated (marriage) separato
serious serio
service (in a restaurant)
  il servizio
**sexually transmitted disease
  (STD)** la malattia sessualmente
  trasmissibile
shampoo lo shampoo
sharp appuntito
shaving cream la crema da barba
sheet (bedlinen) il lenzuolo;
  ~ **(paper)** la pagina
ship v **(mail)** inviare
shirt la camicia
shoes le scarpe; ~ **store** il negozio
  di calzature
shop v fare lo shopping
shopping lo shopping; ~ **area**
  la zona commerciale; ~ **centre**

[BE] il centro commerciale;
  ~ **mall** il centro commerciale
short corto; ~ **sleeves** le maniche
  corte; ~**s** i pantaloncini corti;
  ~**-sighted [BE]** miope
shoulder la spalla
show v mostrare
shower la doccia
shrine il santuario
sick malato
side il lato; ~ **dish** il contorno;
  ~ **effect** l'effetto collaterale;
  ~ **order** il contorno
sightseeing la visita turistica;
  ~ **tour** la gita turistica
sign v firmare
silk la seta
silver l'argento
single (marriage) single;
  ~ **bed** il letto a una piazza;
  ~ **prints** le stampe singole;
  ~ **room** la stanza singola
sink il lavandino
sister la sorella
sit v sedersi
size la taglia
skin la pelle
skirt la gonna
ski v sciare; ~ n lo sci; ~ **lift** lo
  ski lift
sleep v dormire; ~**er car** il vagone

letto; **~ing bag** il sacco a pelo;
~ing car [BE] il vagone letto
slice (of something) la fetta
slippers le ciabatte
slow lento; **~er** più lento;
~ly lentamente
small piccolo; **~er** più piccolo
smoke v fumare
smoking (area) per fumatori
snack bar lo snack bar
sneakers le scarpe da ginnastica
snorkeling equipment
l'attrezzatura da immersione
snow neve; **~board** lo snowboard;
~shoe la scarpa da neve;
~y nevoso
soap il sapone
soccer il calcio
sock il calzino
some qualche
soother [BE] il ciuccio
sore throat il mal di gola
sorry scusi
south sud
souvenir il souvenir; **~ store** il
negozio di souvenir
spa la stazione termale
spatula la spatola
speak v parlare
special (food) la specialità; **~ist
(doctor)** lo specialista

specimen il campione
speeding l'eccesso di velocità
spell v scrivere
spicy piccante
spine (body part) la spina
dorsale
spoon il cucchiaio
sport lo sport; **~s
massage** il massaggio sportivo
sporting goods store il negozio di
articoli sportivi
sprain la storta
square quadrato; **~
kilometer** il chilometro quadrato;
~ meter il metro quadrato
stadium lo stadio
stairs le scale
stamp v **(a ticket)** convalidare;
~ n (postage) il francobollo
start v iniziare
starter [BE] lo starter
station la stazione; **bus ~** la
stazione dei bus; **gas ~** il
benzinaio; **petrol ~ [BE]** il
benzinaio; **railway ~ [BE]** la
stazione ferroviaria; **subway
~** la stazione della metropolitana
train ~ la stazione ferroviaria;
underground ~ [BE] la stazione
della metropolitana;
~ wagon la station wagon

statue la statua
stay v stare
steal v rubare
steep ripido
sterling silver l'argento massiccio
sting la puntura
stolen rubato
stomach lo stomaco; ~**ache** il mal di stomaco
stop v fermarsi; ~ n la fermata
store directory la piantina del negozio
storey [BE] il piano
stove la cucina
straight dritto
strange strano
stream il ruscello
stroller il passeggino
student lo studente
study v studiare
stunning fenomenale
subtitle il sottotitolo
subway la metropolitana; ~ **station** la stazione della metropolitana
suit l'abito; ~**case** la valigia
sun il sole; ~**block** il filtro solare; ~**burn** la scottatura; ~**glasses** gli occhiali da sole; ~**ny** soleggiato; ~**screen** il filtro solare; ~**stroke** l'insolazione

super (fuel) la super; ~**market** il supermercato; ~**vision** la supervisione
surfboard la tavola da surf
swallow v ingoiare
sweater il maglione
sweatshirt la felpa
sweet (taste) dolce; ~**s [BE]** le caramelle
swelling il gonfiore
swim v nuotare; ~**suit** il costume da bagno
symbol (keyboard) il simbolo
synagogue la sinagoga

T

table il tavolo
tablet (medicine) la compressa
take v prendere; ~ **away [BE]** portare via
tampon il tampone
taste v assaggiare
taxi il taxi
team la squadra
teaspoon il cucchiaino
telephone il telefono
temple (religious) il tempio
temporary provvisorio
tennis il tennis
tent la tenda; ~ **peg** il picchetto da tenda; ~ **pole** il paletto da

tenda

terminal (airport) il terminal

terracotta la terracotta

terrible terribile

text *v* **(send a message)** inviare SMS; ~ *n* **(message)** il testo

thank *v* ringraziare; ~ **you** grazie

that che

theater il teatro

theft il furto

there là

thief il ladro

thigh la coscia

thirsty assetato

this questo

throat la gola

ticket il biglietto; ~ **office** la biglietteria; ~**ed passenger** il passeggero con biglietto

tie (clothing) la cravatta

time il tempo; ~**table [BE]** l'orario

tire lo pneumatico

tired stanco

tissue il fazzoletto di carta

tobacconist il tabaccaio

today oggi

toe il dito del piede; ~**nail** l'unghia

toilet [BE] la toilette; ~ **paper** la carta igienica

tomorrow domani

tongue la lingua

tonight stanotte

too troppo

tooth il dente; ~**paste** il dentifricio

total (amount) il totale

tough (food) duro

tourist il turista; ~ **information office** l'ufficio informazioni turistiche

tour la gita

tow truck il carro attrezzi

towel l'asciugamano

tower la torre

town la città; ~ **hall** il municipio; ~ **map** la cartina della città; ~ **square** la piazza della città

toy il giocattolo; ~ **store** il negozio di giocattoli

track (train) il binario

traditional tradizionale

traffic light il semaforo

trail il sentiero; ~ **map** la mappa dei sentieri

trailer la roulotte

train il treno; ~ **station** la stazione ferroviaria

transfer *v* **(change trains/flights)** cambiare; ~ *v* **(money)** trasferire

translate *v* tradurre

trash la spazzatura

travel viaggiare; **~ agency**
l'agenzia viaggi; **~ sickness**
(air) il mal d'aria; **~ sickness**
(car) il mal d'auto; **~ sickness**
(sea) il mal di mare; **~ers**
check il travellers cheque
tree l'albero
trim (hair) una spuntatina
trip il viaggio
trolley [BE] il carrello
trousers i pantaloni
T-shirt la maglietta
turn off v spegnere
turn on v accendere
TV la TV
type v battere a macchina
tyre [BE] lo pneumatico

U

United Kingdom (U.K.) il Regno
Unito
United States (U.S.) gli Stati Uniti
ugly brutto
umbrella l'ombrello
unattended incustodito
unbranded medication [BE]
il farmaco generico
unconscious inconscio
underground [BE]
la metropolitana; **~ station [BE]**
la stazione della metropolitana

underpants le mutande
understand v capire
underwear la biancheria intima
university l'università
unleaded (gas) senza piombo
upper superiore
upset stomach lo stomaco in
disordine
urgent urgente
use v usare
username il nome utente
utensil l'utensile

V

vacancy la disponibilità
vacation la vacanza
vaccination la vaccinazione
vacuum cleaner l'aspirapolvere
vagina la vagina
vaginal infection l'infezione vaginale
valid valido
valley la valle
valuable di valore
value il valore
VAT [BE] l'IVA
vegetarian vegetariano
vehicle registration il numero di
targa
viewpoint la prospettiva
village il villaggio
vineyard il vigneto

visa il visto

visit *v* visitare;

  ~ing hours gli orari di visita

visually impaired ipovedente

vitamin la vitamina

V-neck lo scollo a V

volleyball game la partita di
  pallavolo

vomit *v* vomitare

W

wait *v* attendere; **~** *n* l'attesa;

  ~ing room la sala d'attesa

waiter il cameriere

waitress la cameriera

wake *v* svegliare, svegliarsi;

  ~-up call il servizio sveglia

walk *v* camminare; **~** *n* la
  passeggiata; **~ing route** il
  percorso pedonale

wall clock l'orologio da parete

wallet il portafogli

warm *v* **(something)** riscaldare;
  ~ *adj* **(temperature)** caldo

washing machine la lavatrice

watch l'orologio

water skis lo sci d'acqua

waterfall la cascata

weather il tempo

week la settimana;

  ~end il fine settimana;

  ~ly settimanalmente

welcome *v* accogliere

well-rested ben riposato

west ovest

what (question) cosa

wheelchair la sedia a rotelle; **~**
  ramp la rampa per sedia a rotelle

when (question) quando

where (question) dove

white bianco; **~ gold** l'oro bianco

who (question) chi

widowed vedovo

wife la moglie

window la finestra; **~ case** la
  vetrina

windsurfer il windsurf

wine list la carta dei vini

wireless wireless; **~ internet**
  l'Internet wireless; **~ internet**
  service il servizio Internet wireless;
  ~ phone il telefono cordless

with con

withdraw *v* ritirare; **~al (bank)**
  il prelievo

without senza

woman la donna

wool la lana

work *v* lavorare

wrap *v* incartare

wrist il polso

write *v* scrivere

Y

year l'anno
yellow giallo; **~ gold** l'oro giallo
yes sì
yesterday ieri

young giovane
youth hostel l'ostello della gioventù

Z

zoo lo zoo

Italian–English

A

a buon mercato inexpensive
a destra right (direction)
a girocollo crew neck
a notte per night
a settimana per week
a sinistra left (direction)
a tempo pieno full-time
l'abbazia abbey
l'abbigliamento clothing
abbracciare to hug
l'abito suit
accendere *v* light (cigarette); **~** *v* turn on (lights)
l'accendino lighter
accessibile ai disabili handicapped- [disabled BE] accessible
l'accesso access
accettare *v* accept
accogliere *v* welcome
l'acconciatura hairstyle

l'acconto cash advance
l'acqua water; **~ calda** hot water; **~ potabile** drinking water; **~scooter** jet ski
l'adattatore adapter
addebitare *v* charge (credit card)
l'aereo airplane
l'aeroporto airport
affamato hungry
affittare *v* rent [hire BE]
l'agenzia agency; **~ viaggi** travel agency
l'aggressione attack (on person)
l'agopuntura acupuncture
l'AIDS AIDS
aiutare to help
l'aiuto *n* help
al giorno per day
l'albero tree
all'angolo on the corner
allattare breastfeed
allergico allergic

l'alloggio accommodation
all'ora per hour
alto high
amare *v* love (someone)
l'ambulanza ambulance
americano American
l'amico friend
l'amore *n* love
analcolico non-alcoholic
andare *v* go (somewhere); ~
   bene fit (clothing)
l'andata e ritorno round-trip
l'anello ring
anemico anemic
l'anestesia anesthesia
l'animale animal
l'anno year
annullare *v* cancel
l'antibiotico antibiotic
l'antipasto appetizer [starter BE]
l'anziano senior citizen
aperto *adj* open
l'appartamento apartment
l'appendice appendix (body part)
l'appuntamento appointment
appuntito sharp
l'apribottiglie bottle opener
aprire *v* open
l'apriscatole can opener
arancione orange (color)
l'argento silver; ~ **massiccio**
sterling silver
l'aria condizionata air
   conditioning
l'armadietto locker; ~ **dei bagagli**
   luggage locker
l'aromaterapia aromatherapy
arrivare *v* arrive
arrivederla goodbye
gli arrivi arrivals (airport)
l'arte art
l'arteria artery
gli articoli casalinghi household
   goods
l'artrite arthritis
l'ascensore elevator
l'asciugacapelli hair dryer
l'asciugamano towel
asmatico asthmatic
l'aspirapolvere vacuum cleaner
l'aspirina aspirin
assaggiare *v* taste
l'assegno *n* check (payment)
   [cheque BE]
assetato thirsty
l'assicurazione insurance
l'assorbente sanitary napkin
   [pad BE]
**l'astuccio della macchina
   fotografica** camera case
attendere *v* wait
l'attesa *n* wait

attraente attractive
l'attrattiva attraction (place);
 ~ principale main attraction
l'attrezzatura equipment;
 ~ da immersione snorkeling
 equipment; **~ subacquea** diving
 equipment
gli auricolari headphones
Australia Australia
australiano Australian
l'auto car; **~bus** bus; **~ con il
 cambio automatico** automatic
 car; **~ con il cambio manuale**
 manual car; **~ a noleggio** rental
 [hire BE] car
automatico automatic
l'autonoleggio car rental [hire BE]
l'autostrada highway
 [motorway BE]
avere v have; **~ la nausea** v
 be nauseous
avvertire v notify
l'avvocato lawyer

B

la babysitter babysitter
baciare v kiss
il bagaglio luggage [baggage
 BE]; **~ a mano** carry-on [hand
 luggage BE]
il bagnino lifeguard

il bagno bathroom
ballare v dance
il ballo dancing
il balsamo conditioner
il bambino child
la bambola doll
la banca bank
il bancomat ATM, ATM card, debit
 card
la banconota n bill (money)
 [note BE]
il bar bar; **~ per gay** gay bar
il barbecue barbecue
il barbiere barber
la barca boat; **~ a remi** rowboat
il baseball baseball
il basketball basketball
basso low
i bastoncini cinesi chopsticks
battere a macchina v type
la batteria battery
il bebè baby
beige beige
bello beautiful
il belvedere overlook (scenic place)
ben riposato well-rested
la benda bandage
bene good
la benzina gas (vehicle) [petrol BE]
il benzinaio gas [petrol BE] station
bere v drink

la bevanda *n* drink
la biancheria intima underwear
bianco white
il biberon baby bottle
la biblioteca library
il bicchiere glass (drinking)
la bicicletta bicycle
la biglietteria ticket office
il biglietto ticket; **~ del bus** bus
  ticket; **~ elettronico** e-ticket;
  ~ da visita business card
il bikini bikini
il binario platform; track (train)
blu blue
la bocca mouth
la borsa bag
la borsetta purse [handbag BE]
il bosco forest
la bottiglia bottle
il box playpen
il braccialetto bracelet
il braccio arm
bruciare *v* burn
brutto ugly
la buca delle lettere postbox
buongiorno good morning
buon pomeriggio good afternoon
buonasera good evening
buono *adj* good
il bus espresso express bus
la busta envelope

C

il cabaret cabaret
la cabina cabin
il caffè cafe, coffee
il calcio soccer
caldo hot (temperature)
il calore heat [heating BE]
le calorie calories
il calzino sock
cambiare *v* change; **~** *v* exchange;
  ~ *v* transfer
il cambio *n* change (money);
  ~ *n* exchange (place);
  ~ valuta currency exchange
la cameriera waitress
il cameriere waiter
la camicetta blouse
la camicia shirt
camminare *v* walk
campeggiare *v* camp
il campeggio campsite
il campione specimen
il campo field (sports);
  ~ da golf golf course;
  ~ di battaglia battleground
il Canada Canada
canadese Canadian
il canalone canyon
cancellare *v* clear (on an ATM)
il cane da guida guide dog
i capelli hair

capire v understand
il cappello hat
il cappotto coat
la caraffa carafe
le caramelle candy [sweet BE]
il carbone charcoal
carino cute
caro expensive
il carrello cart [trolley BE];
~ **bagagli** luggage cart
il carro attrezzi tow truck
la carta card, paper;
~ **di credito** credit card;
~ **da cucina** paper towel;
~ **igienica** toilet paper;
~ **d'imbarco** boarding pass;
~ **stagnola** aluminum [kitchen
BE] foil; ~ **dei vini** wine list
la cartina map; ~ **della
città** town map; ~ **delle
piste** trail [piste BE] map;
~ **stradale** road map
la cartolina postcard
il cartone carton
la casa house
la cascata waterfall
il casco helmet
il casinò casino
la cassa case (container);
~**forte** safe (for valuables)
la cassetta della posta mailbox

il cassiere cashier
il castello castle
la cattedrale cathedral
il cavatappi corkscrew
la caviglia ankle
il CD CD
Celsius Celsius
la cena dinner
il centimetro centimeter
il centro downtown area;
~ **business** business center;
~ **commerciale** shopping mall
[centre BE]
la ceramica pottery
la ceretta wax; ~ **all'inguine**
bikini wax; ~ **per sopracciglie**
eyebrow wax
il certificato certificate
il cestino basket (grocery store)
che that
il check-in check-in (hotel/airport)
chi who
chiamare v call
la chiamata n call
la chiave key; ~ **elettronica** key
card; ~ **della stanza** room key
la chiesa church
il chilo kilo; ~**grammo** kilogram;
~**metraggio** mileage;
~**metro** kilometer; ~**metro
quadrato** square kilometer

chiudere *v* close (a shop); ~ *v* lock

chiuso closed

le ciabatte slippers

ciao hi, bye

il cibo food

il ciclismo cycling

il ciclo period (menstrual)

il cinema movie theater

cinese Chinese

la cintura belt

il circuito racetrack

la città town

il ciuccio pacifier [soother BE]

la classe class; ~ **business** business class; ~ **economica** economy class

il club club; ~ **di ballo** dance club; ~ **jazz** jazz club; ~ **per gay** gay club

il codice code; ~ **di abbigliamento** dress code; ~ **PIN** personal identification number (PIN)

la coincidenza connection (flight)

la colazione breakfast

la collana necklace

il collant pantyhose

il collega colleague

il collegamento connection (internet); ~ **wireless a Internet** wireless internet

collegarsi *v* connect (internet)

la collina hill

il collo neck

la colonia cologne

il colore color

il coltello knife

come how

il commissariato police station

la compagnia aerea airline

la compagnia di assicurazione insurance company

compilare *v* fill out (form)

il compleanno birthday

comporre il numero *v* dial

comprare *v* buy

la compressa tablet (medicine)

il computer computer

con with

il concerto concert

la condizione condition (medical)

la conferenza conference

confermare *v* confirm

la congestione congestion

il consolato consulate

il consulente consultant

contagioso contagious

i contanti *n* cash

contattare to contact

il conto *n* bill (of sale); ~ account; ~ **corrente** checking [current BE] account

il contorno side dish
controllare *v* check (luggage)
il controllo passaporti passport control
convalidare *v* stamp (a ticket)
la coperta blanket
il coperto cover charge
la coppa bowl
il corridoio aisle
corto short
cosa what (question)
la coscia thigh
costare *v* cost
costipato constipated
il costo charge (cost)
la costola rib (body part)
il costume da bagno swimsuit
il cotone cotton
il crampo mestruale menstrual cramp
la cravatta tie (clothing)
la crema cream (ointment);
 ~ antisettica antiseptic cream;
 ~ da barba shaving cream
il cristallo crystal
la cuccetta berth
il cucchiaino teaspoon
il cucchiaio spoon
la cucina kitchen, stove
cucinare *v* cook
la culla crib

il cuore heart
il cuscino pillow

D

da banco over the counter (medication)
danneggiare *v* damage
danneggiato damaged
dare *v* give; **~ da mangiare** *v* feed
la data date (calendar)
del pomeriggio p.m.
il denaro money
il dente tooth
la dentiera denture
il dentifricio toothpaste
il dentista dentist
il deodorante deodorant
depositare *v* deposit
il deposito *n* deposit
derubato robbed
il deserto desert
il detersivo detergent;
 ~ per i piatti dishwashing liquid
di fronte a opposite
di valore valuable
diabetico diabetic
il diamante diamond
la diarrea diarrhea
dichiarare *v* declare
il diesel diesel

dietro around (the corner), behind (direction)

difficile difficult

digitale digital

la direzione direction

il disabile handicapped [disabled BE]

la disponibilità vacancy

il disturbo cardiaco heart condition

il dito finger; ~ **del piede** toe

divorziare v divorce

la doccia shower

la dogana customs

dolce sweet (taste)

il dollaro dollar (U.S.)

il dolore hurt (pain); ~ **al petto** chest pain

la domanda question

domani tomorrow

domestico domestic

la donna woman

dopo after; ~**barba** aftershave

doppiato dubbed

dormire v sleep

il dormitorio dormitory

dove where (question)

la dozzina dozen

dritto straight

durante during

duro tough (food)

duty-free duty-free

il DVD DVD

E

l'eccesso excess; ~ **di velocità** speeding

economico cheap

l'edicola newsstand

l'edificio building; ~ **del parlamento** parliament building

l'effetto collaterale side effect

eliminare v delete (computer)

l'e-mail n e-mail

l'emergenza emergency

l'enoteca liquor store [off-licence BE]

entrare v enter

l'entrata entrance

l'erboristeria health food store

l'errore mistake

esausto exhausted

l'escursione excursion; ~ **in pullman** bus tour

esperto expert

espresso express

essere v be

est east

estrarre v extract (tooth)

l'età age

l'euro euro

extra extra; ~ **large** extra large

F

facile easy
la famiglia family
fare v do; **~ l'autostop**
  v hitchhike; **~ la ceretta** v wax;
  ~ un incidente v crash (car);
  ~ il logoff v log off (computer);
  ~ il logon v log on (computer);
  ~ lo shopping v shop;
  ~ le valigie v pack
la farmacia pharmacy [chemist BE]
il fast food fast food
la fattoria farm
la fattura bill [invoice BE]
fatturare v bill (charge)
il fax n fax
il fazzoletto di carta tissue
la febbre fever
il fegato liver (body part)
felice happy
la felpa sweatshirt
fenomenale stunning
fermarsi v stop
la fermata n stop; **~ del bus** bus
  stop
il ferro da stiro n iron (clothes)
la fetta slice (of something)
il fiammifero n match (wooden
  stick)
il film movie
il filtro solare sunblock, sunscreen

il fine settimana weekend
la finestra window
finire v end
il fiore flower
firmare v sign
il fiume river
la fontana fountain
le forbici scissors
la forchetta fork
la foresta pluviale rainforest
il fornello da campeggio
  camping stove
la fortezza fort
la foto photo; **~ digitale** digital
  photo; **~copia** photocopy;
  ~grafia photography
il francobollo n stamp (postage)
il fratello brother
freddo cold (temperature)
il freezer freezer
i freni brakes (car)
frequentare to attend
fresco cool (temperature); **~** fresh
la fretta rush
il frigorifero refrigerator
la frutta e verdura produce
il fruttivendolo grocery store
fumare v smoke
la funivia cable car
il fuoco fire
fuori outside

il furto theft; **~ con scasso** break-in (burglary)

G

la gamba leg
la gara di golf golf tournament
il garage garage
il gas gas (heating);
  ~ per cucina cooking gas
la gastronomia delicatessen
gay gay
il gel gel (hair)
gelato icy
il ghiaccio ice
la giacca jacket
giallo yellow
il giardino botanico botanical
  garden
il ginecologo gynecologist
il ginocchio knee
giocare _v_ play
il giocattolo toy
la gioielleria jewelry
il gioielliere jeweler
il giornale newspaper
il giorno day
giovane young
la gita tour; **~ turistica**
  sightseeing tour
il giubbotto di salvataggio
  life jacket

la giuntura joint (body part)
la goccia drop (medicine)
godersi _v_ enjoy
la gola throat
il gomito elbow
la gomma rubber; **~ a terra**
  flat tire; **~ da masticare**
  chewing gum
il gonfiore swelling
la gonna skirt
i gradi degrees (temperature)
il grammo gram
grande big, large;
  ~ magazzino department store
grazie thank you
grigio gray
la grotta cave
il gruppo group
guardare _v_ look
il guasto breakdown
la guida guide, guide book
guidare _v_ drive

H

l'hockey hockey;
  ~ su ghiaccio ice hockey
l'hotel hotel

I

l'ibuprofene ibuprofen
l'identificazione identification

ieri yesterday
imbarcarsi *v* board
l'impermeabile raincoat
in in; ~ **pensione** retired
incartare *v* wrap
incassare *v* cash
l'incidente accident
incidere *v* engrave
incinta pregnant
includere *v* include
inconscio unconscious
incontrare *v* meet (someone)
l'incontro di boxe boxing match
l'incrocio intersection
incustodito unattended
l'indirizzo address;
   ~ **e-mail** e-mail address
infastidire *v* bother
l'infermiere nurse
infetto infected
l'infezione vaginale vaginal
   infection
le informazioni information
   (phone)
inglese British, English
ingoiare *v* swallow
l'ingresso admission
iniziare *v* begin, start
inserire *v* insert
l'insetto bug
insipido bland

l'insolazione sunstroke
l'insonnia insomnia
l'insulina insulin
interessante interesting
intermedio intermediate
internazionale international
   (airport area)
l'Internet internet; ~ **caffè**
   internet cafe; ~ **wireless** wireless
   internet
l'interno extension (phone)
l'interprete interpreter
l'intestino intestine
intollerante al lattosio lactose
   intolerant
l'intrattenimento
   entertainment
inviare *v* send, ship (mail);
   ~ **e-mail** *v* e-mail; ~ **per fax**
   v fax; ~ **SMS** *v* text (send a
   message)
ipermetrope far- [long- BE]
   sighted
ipovedente visually impaired
l'ippodromo horsetrack
l'Irlanda Ireland
irlandese Irish
l'irritazione rash
l'Italia Italy
italiano Italian
l'IVA sales tax [VAT BE]

J

il jazz jazz
i jeans jeans

L

là there
la casa prefabbricata mobile home
la stanza singola single room
il labbro lip
la lacca hairspray
il ladro thief
il lago lake
la lametta razor blade; **~ usa e getta** disposable razor
la lampadina lightbulb
la lana wool
il latte in polvere formula (baby)
il lato side
la lavanderia laundry; **~ a gettone** laundromat [launderette BE]
il lavandino sink
il lavasecco dry cleaner
la lavastoviglie dishwasher
la lavatrice washing machine
lavorare v work
il lavoro business
lentamente slowly
la lente lens; **~ a contatto** contact lens

il lenzuolo sheet
la lettera letter
il lettino cot
il letto bed; **~ matrimoniale** double bed; **~ a una piazza** single bed
la lezione lesson
libero available, free
la libreria bookstore
il libro book
il lift pass lift pass
la lima nail file
la linea line (train)
la lingua tongue
il lino linen
il litro liter
locale local
lontano far
la lozione lotion
la luce light (overhead)
il lunapark amusement park
lungo long

M

la macchina fotografica camera; **~ digitale** digital camera
il macellaio butcher
la madre mother
la maglietta T-shirt
il maglione sweater
magnifico magnificent

il mal sickness; **~ d'aria** motion sickness (air); **~ d'auto** motion sickness (car); **~ di gola** sore throat; **~ di mare** motion sickness (sea); **~ d'orecchio** earache; **~ di schiena** backache; **~ di stomaco** stomachache; **~ di testa** headache

malato sick [ill BE]

malattia sessualmente trasmissibile sexually transmitted disease (STD)

mancante missing

mangiare v eat

le maniche sleeves; **~ corte** short sleeves; **~ lunghe** long sleeves

il manicure manicure

la mano hand

il mare sea

il marito husband

marrone brown

il martello hammer

la mascella jaw

il massaggio massage; **~ sportivo** sports massage

il mattino morning

del mattino a.m.

il meccanico mechanic

la medicina medicine

il medico doctor

medio medium (size)

meno less

il menù menu; **~ delle bevande** drink menu; **~ per bambini** children's menu

il mercato market

le merci goods

il mese month

la messa mass (church service)

il messaggio message; **~ istantaneo** instant message

la metà half

il metro quadrato square meter

la metropolitana subway [underground BE]

la mezz'ora half hour

la mezzanotte midnight

il mezzo chilo half-kilo

mezzogiorno noon [midday BE]

il microonde microwave

migliore better

il migliore best

il minibar mini-bar

il minuto minute

miope near- [short- BE] sighted

misurare v measure (someone, something)

il misurino measuring spoon

mobile mobile

la mobilità mobility

i mocassini loafers

il mocio mop
modificare *v* alter (clothing)
il modulo form (fill-in)
la moglie wife
la moneta coin
la montagna mountain
il monumento memorial (place)
la moschea mosque
mostrare *v* show
la motocicletta motorcycle
il motore motor
il motoscafo motor boat
la mountain bike mountain bike
la mousse mousse (hair)
la multa fine (fee for breaking law)
il municipio town hall
il muscolo muscle
il museo museum
la musica music; ~ **classica** classical music; ~ **folk** folk music; ~ **pop** pop music
le mutande underpants

N

il naso nose
il nastro trasportatore conveyor belt
le natiche buttocks
la nazionalità nationality
necessitare *v* need

il negozio store; ~ **d'abbigliamento** clothing store; ~ **d'antiquariato** antique store; ~ **di articoli da regalo** gift shop; ~ **di articoli sportivi** sporting goods store; ~ **di calzature** shoe store; ~ **di fotografia** camera store; ~ **di giocattoli** toy store; ~ **di musica** music store; ~ **di souvenir** souvenir store
nero black
la neve snow
nevoso snowy
niente nothing
il nightclub nightclub
il nipote grandchild
no no
noioso boring
il nome name; ~ **utente** username
non fumatori non-smoking
il nonno grandparent
nord north
normale regular
la notte night
il numero number; ~ **di fax** fax number; ~ **di patente** driver's license number; ~ **di targa** vehicle registration; ~ **di telefono** phone number
nuotare *v* swim

O

gli occhiali glasses;
  ~ da sole sunglasses
l'occhio eye
oggi today
OK OK
l'olio oil
l'ombrello umbrella
l'opera opera
ora now
l'ora hour
gli orari di visita visiting hours
l'orario schedule [timetable BE];
  ~ d'apertura business hours;
  ~ d'ufficio office hours
l'orchestra orchestra
ordinare v order
gli orecchini earrings
l'orecchio ear
l'oro gold;
  ~bianco white gold;
  ~ giallo yellow gold
l'orologio watch;
  ~ da parete wall clock
l'ospedale hospital
l'osso bone
l'ostello hostel; **~ della
  gioventù** youth hostel
l'ottico optician
l'otturazione filling (tooth)
ovest west

P

il pacchetto package
la padella frying pan
il padre father
il pagamento del conto check-out
  (hotel)
pagare v pay
il palazzo palace
la palestra gym
il paletto da tenda tent pole
la panetteria bakery
il pannolino diaper [nappy BE]
i pantaloncini corti shorts
i pantaloni pants [trousers BE]
il paracetamolo acetaminophen
  [paracetamol BE]
parcheggiare v park
il parcheggio parking garage;
  ~ parking lot [car park BE]
il parco n park; **~ giochi**
  playground
parlare v speak
il parrucchiere hair salon
le partenze departures (airport)
partire v leave
la partita game, match; **~ di
  football** soccer [football game
  BE]; **~ di pallavolo** volleyball
  game
part-time part-time
il passaggio lift

il passaporto passport

passare v pass through

il passeggero passenger; **~ con biglietto** ticketed passenger

la passeggiata n walk

il passeggino stroller [pushchair BE]

la password password

la pasticceria pastry shop

il pasto meal

il pediatra pediatrician

il pedicure pedicure

il pedone pedestrian

la pelle leather, skin

la pellicola per alimenti plastic wrap [cling film BE]

il peltro pewter

il pene penis

la penicillina penicillin

la penna pen

la pensione bed and breakfast

la pentola saucepan, pot

per for, per; **~ favore** please; **~ fumatori** smoking (area); **~ la notte** overnight

il percorso route; **~ alternativo** alternate route; **~ ciclabile** bike route; **~ pedonale** walking route

perdere v lose (something)

la perdita discharge (bodily fluid)

pericoloso dangerous

il periodo period (of time)

la perla pearl

permettere v allow, permit

perso lost

il pettine comb

il petto chest (body part)

il petto breast

il pezzo piece

piacere v like

il piacere pleasure

il piano floor [storey BE]

il pianterreno ground floor

la piantina del negozio store directory

il piatto plate; **~ principale** main course

la piazza della città town square

piccante hot (spicy)

il picchetto da tenda tent peg

piccolo little, petite, small

il piede foot

il pigiama pajamas

la pillola Pill (birth control)

la pioggia rain

piovoso rainy

la piscina pool; **~ per bambini** kiddie [paddling BE] pool; **~ esterna** outdoor pool; **~ interna** indoor pool

pista piste [BE]

più more; **~ basso** lower;
~ economico cheaper; **~ forte**
louder; **~ grande** bigger; **~ lento**
slower; **~ piccolo** smaller;
~ tardi later; **~ veloce** faster
la pizzeria pizzeria
il pizzo lace
il platino platinum
lo pneumatico tire [tyre BE]
la polizia police
il polmone lung
il polso wrist
il pomeriggio afternoon
la pompa dell'aria air pump
il ponte bridge
la porta door; **~ antincendio** fire
door
il portachiavi key ring
il portafogli wallet
portare *v* bring; **~ indietro**
v return (something); **~ via** to go
[take away BE]
la porzione portion; **~ per
bambini** children's portion
la posa exposure (film)
la posta *n* mail [post BE];
~ aerea airmail
il posto seat; **~ sul corridoio** aisle
seat
il pranzo lunch
la precedenza right of way

il prefisso area code; **~ del
paese** country code
il prelievo withdrawal (bank)
prendere *v* take
prenotare *v* reserve
la prenotazione reservation
la presa elettrica electric outlet
prescrivere *v* prescribe
presentare *v* introduce
il preservativo condom
la pressione sanguigna
blood pressure
presto early
la previsione forecast
il prezzo price
prima before, earlier;
~ classe first class
primo first
il principiante beginner, novice
il problema problem
i prodotti per la pulizia cleaning
supplies
profondamente deeply
il profumo perfume
il programma *n* schedule
programmare *v* schedule
proibire *v* prohibit
pronto ready
pronunciare *v* pronounce
la prospettiva viewpoint
prossimo next

provvisorio temporary
pubblico public
pulire *v* clean
pulito *adj* clean
la pulizia del viso facial
la puntura sting; **~ d'insetto** insect bite

Q

quadrato square
qualche some
la qualità quality
qualsiasi cosa anything
quando when (question)
quanto how much (question)
questo this
qui here

R

la racchetta racket (sports)
le racchette poles (skiing)
raccogliere *v* pick up (something)
raccomandare *v* recommend
la raccomandata registered mail
la raccomandazione recommendation
il radiatore heater
il raffreddore cold (sickness)
la ragazza girl, girlfriend
il ragazzo boy, boyfriend
raggiungere *v* reach (get hold of)

il rame copper
la rampa per sedia a rotelle wheelchair ramp
il rap rap (music)
la reazione allergica allergic reaction
la reception reception
il reclamo complaint
il regalo gift
il reggiseno bra
la regione region
il Regno Unito United Kingdom (U.K.)
la relazione relationship
il rene kidney (body part)
il repellente per gli insetti insect repellent
il residente UE EU resident
respirare *v* breathe
il ricambio part (for car)
il riciclaggio *n* recycling
la ricetta prescription
ricevere *v* receive
la ricevuta receipt
il riciclaggio *n* recycling
riempire *v* fill
rifiutare *v* decline (credit card)
ringraziare *v* thank
riparare *v* fix, mend, repair
ripetere *v* repeat
ripido steep

il responsabile manager
il riscaldamento heating
riscaldare v warm (something)
la riserva naturale nature preserve
i risparmi savings (account)
il ristorante restaurant
ritardare v delay
ritirare v withdraw
il ritiro bagagli baggage claim
la riunione meeting
la rivista magazine
romantico romantic
rompere v break
rosa pink
rosso red
rotto broken
la roulotte trailer
le rovine ruins
rubare v rob, steal
rubato stolen
il rugby rugby
il rullino film (camera)
il ruscello stream

S

il sacchetto per i rifiuti garbage
[rubbish BE] bag
il sacco a pelo sleeping bag
la sala room; ~ **congressi**
convention hall; ~ **d'attesa**
waiting room; ~ **da concerti**
concert hall; ~ **da pranzo** dining
room; ~ **giochi** arcade;
~ **riunioni** meeting room
il salone di bellezza nail salon
la salute health
Salute! Cheers!
salvare v save (computer)
salve hello
la salvietta per neonati baby
wipe
i sandali sandals
il sangue blood
sanguinare v bleed
il santuario shrine
il sapone soap
la sauna sauna
la sbornia hangover
le scale stairs; ~
mobili escalators
lo scanner scanner
le scarpe shoes;
~ **da neve** snowshoes;
~ **basse** flat shoes; ~ **col tacco
alto** high-heeled shoes;
~ **da ginnastica** sneakers
gli scarponi da montagna hiking
boots
la scatola box
lo scatolame canned good
scendere v get off (a train, bus,
subway)

la scheda card; **~ memoria** memory card; **~ telefonica** phone card

lo schermo display

la schiena back (body part)

lo sci *n* ski; **~ d'acqua** water skis

sciare *v* ski

la sciarpa scarf

la scienza science

scippare *v* mug

la scogliera cliff

la scolapasta colander

scollegare *v* disconnect (computer)

lo scollo a V V-neck

scommettere *v* place a bet

scomparso missing

lo sconto discount

lo scontrino bagagli luggage [baggage BE] ticket

lo scooter moped

la scopa broom

la scottatura sunburn

scrivere *v* spell, write

la scuola school

scuro dark

scusare *v* excuse

scusi sorry (apology)

sedersi *v* sit

la sedia chair; **~ a rotelle** wheelchair; **~ a sdraio** deck chair

il sedile per bambino child's seat

il seggiolino per auto car seat

il seggiolone highchair

la seggiovia chair lift

il self-service self-service

il semaforo traffic light

il seminario seminar

il senso unico one-way street

il sentiero path, trail

senza without; **~ grassi** fat free; **~ piombo** unleaded (gas)

separato separated (marriage)

la sera evening

serio serious

la serratura *n* lock

i servizi di pulizia domestica housekeeping services

il servizio service (in a restaurant); **~ completo** full-service; **~ di lavanderia** laundry service; **~ in camera** room service; **~ Internet** internet service; **~ Internet wireless** wireless internet service; **~ sveglia** wake-up call

la seta silk

la settimana week

settimanalmente weekly

lo shampoo shampoo

lo shopping shopping

sì yes

la sicurezza security

sicuro safe (protected)
la sigaretta cigarette
il sigaro cigar
il simbolo symbol (keyboard)
la sinagoga synagogue
single single (marriage)
lo ski lift drag lift, ski lift
lo slip briefs (clothing)
lo smalto enamel (jewelry)
lo snack bar snack bar
lo snowboard snowboard
il sole sun
soleggiato sunny
solo alone, only; ~ **andata** one-way (ticket)
la soluzione per lenti a contatto contact lens solution
la sonnolenza drowsiness
sopra over
sordo deaf
la sorella sister
il sottotitolo subtitle
il souvenir souvenir
la spalla shoulder
la spatola spatula
la spazzatura trash [rubbish BE]
la spazzola hairbrush
lo specialista specialist (doctor)
la specialità special (food)
spedire v mail
spegnere v turn off (lights)

lo spettacolo n play (theater); ~ **di danza** ballet
la spiaggia beach
la spilla brooch
la spina dorsale spine (body part)
spingere v push (door sign)
lo spogliatoio fitting room
sporco dirty
lo sport sport
sposare v marry
sposato married
la spuntatina trim (hair)
la squadra team
squisito delicious
lo stadio stadium
lo stagno pond
stampare v print
la stampa n print; ~ **digitale** digital print; ~ **singola** single print
stanco tired
stanotte tonight
la stanza room
stare v stay
gli Stati Uniti United States (U.S.)
la station wagon station wagon [estate car BE]
la statua statue
la stazione station; ~ **degli autobus** bus station; ~ **dei bus**

bus station; **~ ferroviaria** train station [railway station BE]; **~ della metropolitana** subway station [underground station BE]; **~ di servizio** gas station [petrol station BE]; **~ termale** spa

la stecca di sigarette carton of cigarettes

le sterline pounds (British sterling)

stesso same

stirare *v* iron, press (clothing)

gli stivali boots

lo stomaco stomach; **~ in disordine** upset stomach

stordito dizzy

la storta sprain

strano strange

straordinario amazing

lo studente student

studiare *v* study

stuprare *v* rape

lo stupro *n* rape

lo sturalavandini plunger

sud south

la super super (fuel)

superiore upper

il supermercato supermarket

la supervisione supervision

svegliare, svegliarsi *v* wake

sviluppare *v* develop (film)

svuotare *v* empty

T

il tabaccaio tobacconist

la taglia size; **~ forte** plus size

tagliare *v* cut (hair)

il taglio *n* cut (injury), haircut

il tampone tampon

tardi late (time)

la tariffa fee

la tasca pocket

la tassa duty (tax)

il tasso di cambio exchange rate

la tavola da surf surfboard

il tavolo table

il taxi taxi

la tazza cup; **~ di misurazione** measuring cup

il teatro theater; **~ dell'opera** opera house

telefonare *v* phone

la telefonata phone call

il telefonino cell [mobile BE] phone

il telefono *n* phone; **~ telephone; ~ cordless** wireless phone; **~ pubblico** pay phone

il telone impermeabile groundcloth [groundsheet BE]

il tempio temple (religious)

il tempo time, weather

la tenda tent

il tennis tennis

la terapia ad ossigeno oxygen treatment

le terme hot spring

il terminal terminal (airport)

la terracotta terracotta

terribile terrible

la tessera card; **~ associativa** membership card; **~ dell'assicurazione** insurance card; **~ internazionale dello studente** international student card

la testa head (body part)

il testo *n* text (message)

tirare *v* pull (door sign)

la toilette restroom [toilet BE]

la torcia elettrica flashlight

la torre tower

la tosse *n* cough

tossire *v* cough

il totale total (amount)

il tovagliolo napkin

tradizionale traditional

tradurre *v* translate

il traghetto ferry

tranquillo quiet

trasferire *v* transfer (money)

il travellers cheque travelers check [travelers cheque BE]

il treno train; **~ espresso** express train

triste sad

troppo too

tuffarsi *v* dive

il turista tourist

la TV TV

U

l'uccello bird

l'ufficio office; **~ di cambio** currency exchange office; **~ informazioni** information desk; **~ informazioni turistiche** tourist information office; **~ oggetti smarriti** lost and found; **~ postale** post office; **~ prenotazioni** reservation desk

ultimo last

una volta once

l'unghia fingernail, toenail

unire *v* join

l'università university

uno one

l'uomo man

urgente urgent

usa e getta disposable

usare *v* use

uscire *v* exit

l'uscita gate (airport), exit; **~ d'emergenza** emergency exit

l'utensile utensil

V

la vacanza vacation [holiday BE]
la vaccinazione vaccination
la vagina vagina
il vagone letto sleeper [sleeping BE] car
valido valid
la valigia suitcase
la valle valley
il valore value
la valuta currency
il vaso jar
vecchio old
vedere v see
vedovo widowed
vegetariano vegetarian
il veleno poison
veloce fast
vendere v sell
venire v come
il ventaglio fan (souvenir)
il ventilatore fan (appliance)
il verbale di polizia police report
verde green
vero real
la vescica bladder
il vestito dress (piece of clothing)
la vetrina window case
la vetrinetta display case
il vetro glass (material)

la vetta peak (of a mountain)
il viaggio trip
vicino close, near, nearby, next to
i vigili del fuoco fire department
il vigneto vineyard
il villaggio village
viola purple
la visita turistica sightseeing
visitare v visit
il viso face
il visto visa
la vita life
la vitamina vitamin
vivere v live
il volo flight; ~ **internazionale** international flight; ~ **nazionale** domestic flight
vomitare v vomit

W

il WC da campeggio chemical toilet
il windsurf windsurfer

Z

lo zaino backpack
la zona area; ~ **commerciale** shopping area; ~ **picnic** picnic area
lo zoo zoo

Berlitz®

speaking your language

phrase book & dictionary
phrase book & CD

Available in: Arabic, Cantonese Chinese, Croatian, Czech, Danish, Dutch, English*, Finnish*, French, German, Greek, Hebrew*, Hindi, Hungarian*, Indonesian, Italian, Japanese, Korean, Latin American Spanish, Mandarin Chinese, Mexican Spanish, Norwegian, Polish, Portuguese, Romanian*, Russian, Spanish, Swedish, Thai, Turkish, Vietnamese

*Book only

www.berlitzpublishing.com